Where Is Your Treasure?

THOUGHTS TO AWAKEN, COMFORT AND INSPIRE

AMBASSADOR

BELFAST, NORTHERN IRELAND
GREENVILLE, USA

Where Is Your Treasure?

THOUGHTS TO AWAKEN, COMFORT AND INSPIRE

Chris Jewell

AMBASSADOR

BELFAST, NORTHERN IRELAND
GREENVILLE, USA

Where Is Your Treasure? Thoughts to Awaken, Comfort and Inspire
© Copyright 2001 Chris Jewell

ISBN 1   84030 113 9

Ambassador Publications
a division of
Ambassador Productions Ltd.
Providence House
Ardenlee Street,
Belfast,
BT6 8QJ
Northern Ireland
www.ambassador-productions.com

Emerald House
427 Wade Hampton Blvd.
Greenville
SC 29609, USA
www.emeraldhouse.com

Preface

This book has its origins from an approach my father, Brian Jewell, made to the *Greenock Telegraph*, his local evening newspaper in the West of Scotland, some twenty years ago when he was in his sixties and not keeping in the best of health.

My father had been active in Christian work since his conversion in the 1960s and travelled both locally and further afield to take or be involved in Christian meetings. With poorer health and not being out and about so often, he felt that with a regular Christian column in the *Greenock Telegraph*, he would be able to reach a much larger number of people than previously.

His first approach was turned down as it was not thought to be the kind of thing that would be appropriate for the paper. However, some three months later the *Telegraph* agreed to his proposal and so began a weekly series of articles in the Saturday editions of the paper, under the title 'Thought for Today' and published on an anonymous basis.

The column prospered and received encouraging feedback from time to time. Dad wrote fluently and easily. His health, however, continued to deteriorate and in March 1984 he returned to the South of England, the area of his upbringing, and continued writing from there.

Dad died in May 1984, having completed 228 'Thought for Today' articles. My older brother Derek and I talked about continuing the column and we both produced a number of examples in a similar style which were accepted by the *Telegraph*, and so the weekly 'Thought for Today' column continued uninterrupted in the paper.

In October 1985, Derek died, suddenly, with little warning. As a boy he had suffered from ulcerated colitis, then and still now a dangerous disease, and had undergone many surgical operations over the years. He and I had become Christians in our late teens, but his liver had suffered severe damage as a result of his illnesses and then in his late thirties it gave out on him. After his death, I continued writing the column myself and it has been this way since 1985. There have now been over 1,100 Thought for Today articles published in the *Telegraph* and they continue to appear each Saturday.

In recent years I considered the idea of producing a selection of these articles for a wider audience and discussed matters from time to time with Sam Lowry of Ambassador Productions in Belfast. 'Where Is Your Treasure?' is the result of these discussions.

This little book is published in memory both of Dad and of Derek, whose wife and children are deeply involved in Christian ministry today. I am grateful to Stewart Anderson who initially encouraged me to proceed with a book, and also to the *Greenock Telegraph* for permission to use the original articles which have been adapted somewhat.

Thanks are also due to my mother Phyllis Jewell, the late Mr. Hugh Black and his daughter Alison for their practical help and support and to Kristeen Bell for her help in producing the final manuscript.

Many of the articles published in this book are drawn from ordinary day to day examples of life, which mirror a number of very real Christian principles. When we come to Christ and personally commit our life and future to Him, we no longer live ordinary lives, but the miraculous life of God lives in us. He makes openings where we see no ways through, He makes the impossible the actual, and there is no greater place to be than in the warmth and loveliness of His presence.

It is my real hope that you will find the full nature of the marvellous treasure described in this book, treasure that is there for each one of us.

Chris Jewell
September 2001

• *Scriptures quoted are from the Authorised (King James) Version of the Bible.*

Contents

A Common Purpose

We take our caravan with us on holiday from time to time, and enjoy the use of it at a number of sites. Returning home on one occasion we left the caravan outside our front gate as our driveway is on a fairly steep slope and I thought that I might need help in manoeuvring it back into its usual position. And so it proved.

Firstly, I tried reversing it up the hill and over the pavement, but only succeeded in burning out the clutch of my car and having to replace it. Ouch! Then, with the help of relatives, we tried to push it, but didn't get very far. And so it remained outside the front gate until a better solution arrived a few days later.

With the help of a few strong men who were working nearby, we had no difficulty at all, and with no danger to our hernias, in pushing the caravan up the hill, over the pavement and up the driveway into position. It only took a few moments, and no sweat. I reflected upon how easy it had been with their help, and about all the various unsuccessful efforts I had previously made.

One man on his own had been no good, even in his car. One or two more weren't enough to make an impact. And if there had been many men, but they all were pushing in different directions, we still wouldn't have got there. But a good number of us, all helping each other and pushing and pulling together, got the job done.

In our work for Jesus Christ and His Kingdom, we need to work together for good – there are many occasions where a number of us are needed. But if we're all pulling in different directions, we should not expect the desired result. When even a few are working and pulling together under the direction of the Holy Spirit, results happen.

For we are labourers together with God.
1 Corinthians 3:9

13

A Cry For Help

Our cat is one who tends to come and go about the house as she pleases with the aid of a cat flap. One evening, she had gone out but this time by a different route. She had squeezed out through a slightly open upstairs window, onto the window ledge, then jumped down some three feet to a wider ledge below, but still some 15 feet above the ground. Along this ledge she travelled, then jumped across a three-foot gap in it to our next-door neighbours' part of the building, then up three feet to the neighbours' window ledge to the same height as the one she went through at the beginning of this journey.

There was one difference though. The neighbours' window was shut. And because it was a sealed double glazed unit and couldn't be opened, the cat had effectively reached a dead end, and would have to reverse her journey to gain access again to her home. However, it was darker now and coming back was not as easy as it had been getting there.

After a while, her meows for help were heard by our neighbours. After unsuccessfully encouraging the cat to come back along her route, we were left with having to call the fire brigade who came with a long ladder and rescued her. I reckon that's another of her nine lives she's used up.

Many of us set out on a route which we think will bring us all we want in life, be it success, wealth, fame or happiness. And we find after a while that our route too has taken us to a dead end and it looks impossible to return. Indeed, maybe you are at your dead end right now, with no seeming way out. You need a rescuer too and Christ stands before you with arms outstretched to save. You can trust Him to take you from where you are and set your feet on the right path.

I would seek unto God, and unto God would I commit my cause.
Job 5:8

Aflame With Him

A friend of ours was telling us of a visit he, his wife and baby son made to some friends. In the house was a coal fire which, when they arrived, was at a low ebb with only the embers to be seen.

During the course of their visit, the hosts put some more coal on the fire, which then began to flare up with flames burning brightly. The baby boy, who had not noticed the embers at all, suddenly saw the flames begin to appear and was captivated by it all. Despite other attractions (or distractions), he remained captivated by the flames as they danced above the coals. It was obviously so much more interesting than the embers had been.

We hear a lot, if we listen to Christian teaching or preaching, about the Church being likened to coals of fire ... or is it dying embers? God intends that His Church - that's you and me if we are believers - should be aflame with life and vigour, on fire for Him, not barely alive as an ember. He's looking for a mighty conflagration from us all so bright and powerful that we will certainly be noticed ... burning with His life within us.

So if your life is but an ember, the one good thing about being an ember is that you are capable of greater things. With the wind of the Holy Spirit upon you and fuelled by His love and His passion to win others, you will burn brightly in the days to come, drawing others to Him.

Set yourself to seek for the power of the fire of God to come upon you. Open yourself to His energising. Become aflame for Him.

And they said one to another, Did not our heart burn within us,
while he talked with us by the way, and while he opened to us
the scriptures?
Luke 24:32

Aim High

Many of us will be familiar with the saying 'You are what you want to be', although we might not entirely agree with its sentiments. We argue that our personal background, lack of talent or wealth, or both, is such that there are many things or people we might want to be, but have no earthly hope of achieving it. And I would have to agree that, where the material things of life are concerned, you are probably right.

But when it comes to our personalities, our 'inner selves' and our spiritual lives, the same restrictions do not hold true; we are all born with the same potential in these things.

To use another phrase, when it comes to Christ's call on our lives, 'the sky's the limit.' There are no restrictions – only ourselves. We will be, in practice, what we want to be.

If we are ready to dedicate our lives in Christ's service, and live in that light, our lives will be fruitful for Him. If, however, we see the Christian life as one of only toil, trouble and trying to avoid temptations, then the chances are it will turn out that way. If we believe that we are not equipped to be what God wants us to be, and do not allow Him to change us, then we'll probably live our lives with very small horizons.

Should you already be walking the Christian road, don't let your shoulders droop, your head hang down or your spirits fall. He is with you, waiting to lift you and recharge you, and to deal with anything that would hinder your walk with Him. Lift up your head, lift up your hands and make your horizons large and wide – the way is already made for you.

I will lift mine eyes unto the hills, from whence cometh my help.
Psalm 121:1

And The First Shall Be Last

Travelling in the car, listening to the sports news on the radio I heard how yet another football manager had lost his job. This time it was due to a new boss arriving and not wanting his services; usually it is a run of poor results on the park which spell the death knell for the manager ... and often, it seems, just after he has had a public vote of confidence from his board of directors!

Everything seems to be about winning and coming first. Everyone just has to come first, which of course is absurd, as only ever one team can come first, unless there is a tie.

It's true of business too. It seems to be all about being the biggest and the best. 'You are only as good as your last results' is a remark I've heard employees complain about in increasing numbers these days.

Of course it's mostly to do with money and success. But Jesus said it somewhat differently. 'The last shall be first and the first shall be last.' The things we all generally strive for, or our earthly masters make us strive for, are not the things that will matter at the end of the day. I think the humble soul who may not have the biggest job, or the fanciest car, or have made the highest shareholder returns for his company, but who has followed Jesus with sincerity and humility and a longing for God will end up amongst the first when it comes to the kingdom of heaven.

And those of us who have put wealth, power, lust, or earthly ambition ahead of our desire to follow the Son of God may find that we are at the bottom of the heap at the end of the day.

The choices we make decide our fate.

But many that are first shall be last, and the last first.
Mark 10:31

A New Beginning

I am sure that many of us can remember a time when we wished to start something over again. Whether it was an exam at school or college, our first words to our new boss, a letter applying for a new job, or our first day at one, we will remember wishing we could change it all and start again.

Maybe we have had an argument with someone we love and said words in the heat of the moment that we wish we hadn't. Or completely fallen out with them. Maybe we've done something we're deeply ashamed about and wish we could turn the clock back to before it happened.

The coming of Easter is about new beginnings. It's about wiping the slate clean, and rubbing out all that's gone before. It's about starting out afresh.

As the well-known hymn puts it, 'There was none other good enough to pay the price of sin; He only could unlock the gates of heaven and let us in.'

On that green hill far away, outside the city wall, something miraculous took place. Something that would last forever. Something on so vast a scale that we cannot even begin to imagine it and its consequences. Three men were crucified … one of them was the Son of God.

He had done nothing wrong; indeed He had done so much good. Yet He knew that this one act of obedience and of sacrifice would set men and women free forever. Once and for all, Jesus paid the price for your and my sinning. We can go free of its condemnation, free of its shame and of its guilt. Get your mind round that – it's stupendous.

Easter is not about our failures of the past, it's about His triumph and our hope for the future. If you are in need of a new beginning, here is where you find it. Recognise Jesus for who He is, know that He died for you and accept His offer of forgiveness. You'll be a different person and that first Easter will mark a new beginning for you.

A new heart also will I give you, and a new spirit will I put within you: and I will take away the stony heart out of your flesh, and I will give you an heart of flesh.
Ezekiel 36:26

&

A Recipe For Success

&

I'm not much of a chef. I've never had any professional training, although I am able to produce one or two fairly simple dishes if called upon to do so with my specialities being nothing more than scrambled eggs or toad-in-the-hole.

Food, of course, is a basic human need, essential to our human survival. But there will be few of us who cannot be charmed by the sound of an exotic dish, described with almost loving care, and brimming with superlatives, by an excited and experienced cook. Even the way they say 'succulent' can get the taste buds going.

And it works, at least in the affluent parts of the world, judging by the amounts of money and time people spend in expensive restaurants, often supported by previously fattened expense accounts!

There is another recipe for us but not one where the end product is a delicate dessert or a succulent roast. It doesn't consider your appetite but your inner person, the real you.

What about a recipe which leads to deep inner peace and contentment; freedom from fear and its family friends of nervousness, anxiety and worry; a new purpose in life and a satisfaction that cannot be equalled by any earthly dish, however grand its description and exquisite its taste?

A recipe for overcoming, for victory and for the energy that is harnessed within a turned-around life. It comes from only one source. The living Christ – the Son of God, Jesus.

If our hearts on hearing of Jesus are quickened to want to know Him and find this peace and contentment as well as His power and His love, then the recipe is to turn ourselves towards Him, seek Him out and exchange our life for His own within us.

There's no better recipe for today, tomorrow, next week or forever.

I am the bread of life.
John 6:48

&

Back To Basics

&

At the time it was announced, we heard quite a lot about the British Government's 'Back to Basics' policy and campaign, but I do not hear much about it these days.

Yet there is a truth about the need to get back to basics, when things have gone wrong or come unstuck. There's no point in designing a fabulous looking new car with futuristic lines, if the basic engine design is faulty and the car is unreliable. The best looking furniture will not sell well or do its job if the hinges or screws start to come out after only a short time.

It's true also of our relationship and our walk with God. If we are out of touch with Him, or have never been in touch with Him, we need to get back to the basics.

Basic truths like the fact that our sin separates us from God and keeps us from Him. Sin also destroys our peace with God. Sin corrupts. Sin hurts both us and those around us. And sin seeks to destroy our potential for God. Sin has many names - cheating, stealing, jealousy, hatred, to name a few.

Not a pleasant tale is it? And there are many today who have proved it so, some walking in what to them is a 'living hell.' If you've wandered or not listened to the voice of God and His Holy Spirit speaking to you, you need to get back to basics. Back to the place of repentance until your hear His voice of forgiveness, back to the place where He comes first, and where our trust is fully in Him.

Don't be deceived by all the flashy talk that's about these days. Talk of self-discovery, of self-awareness, of self-fulfilment. It's not talk of self we need, it's of God and His righteousness. That's worth talking about and will set us free.

I have blotted out, as a thick cloud, thy transgressions, and, as a
cloud, thy sins: return unto me, for I have redeemed thee.
Isaiah 44:22

Barrenness

A fter a gap of some years, I went back to a very well known estate in the countryside, walking alongside what had once been a small building. All that was now left was the concrete floor.

The place had a very barren look about it with all kinds of weeds sprouting through the concrete as nature endeavoured to take over the site once again. It was sad to see the dereliction for I had fond memories associated with the building that had once stood there.

Is our life one that started well for God where we have known His anointing and His presence but for whatever reasons we have allowed ourselves to drift from the sharpness of His ways and the clarity of His speaking? Have the clear pathways to God which were created as part of our walking with Him become unused and covered again with weeds and other plants which speak of wrong doing and other weaknesses?

If so, it's time to retrace our steps and renew our contact with God. It may mean throwing out a lot that has come into our lives and attitudes. It may be deeper than that and we need God to deal with whatever has become between Him and us. It will call for His forgiveness and mercy but the wonderful thing is that God is ever ready to receive one of His children who has erred, realised it and determined to return to Him. God's arms are outstretched to receive and welcome a returning son or daughter.

And I will give them a heart to know me, that I am the Lord: and
they shall be my people, and I will be their God: for they shall
return unto me with their whole heart.
Jeremiah 24:7

Beautiful Within

S ome years ago, one of our national daily papers described the latest 'revolutionary' pills, which if taken in the morning and in the evening, claimed to radically improve your looks and increase your beauty.

The pills turned out to include a fairly normal mixture of vitamins and herbs with no magic ingredients. The paper went on to give 10 useful tips to help you look vibrant and beautiful, with none of them including the need to take pills.

Many of us are rather concerned about the way we look, and spend a lot of effort and money trying to ensure that we look our best. Now there's nothing wrong, I suggest, in wanting to look your best, but there's a lot more to it than our skin tones and healthy hair (assuming your head still has some!).

It's much more to do with our character, how we react, how we care for one another, how we refuse to take offence, how we deal with the difficulties that life puts in front of us. If the love of God is in a person, that love flows out through them ... through their eyes, their faces, their actions, their care and concern for their fellows. There comes a special light from them, which is so much richer than anything the latest skin cream or pill can do.

God is interested in the core that is us, rather than outward appearances, which can be so deceiving. His own life within us will bring about dramatic, life changing results far beyond anything else.

I am the light of the world: he that followeth me shall not walk in
darkness, but shall have the light of life.
John 8:12

Being Clean

Not many of us would want to stay in the same set of clothes day after day, week after week, month after month. And none of us would wish a member of the family, relative, friend, indeed anyone we came into contact with to do the same!

For layer upon layer of dust would settle on our clothing and build up on each item, clogging the fabrics, and getting them dirtier and dirtier. And that's only on the outside! On the inside, the sweat and warmth we give out would be retained within our clothing. Not a pretty picture is it?

So we change and wash both ourselves and our clothing regularly. But what about the same principle where our spiritual lives are concerned?

How often do we have the inner person cleansed? Cleansed of that angry word, bitter thought, lustful look, act of violence or foolishness, as well as the more well known sins – for they all hang on to us like dust gathers and clings to our clothes.

We need to be clean on the inside just as often as on the outside. And the Bible tells us that if we come and confess our sins, Jesus will forgive them.

If you have need to be clean and to be rid of the iniquity that is on you and your life, come to Jesus now and let Him touch you and make you completely clean.

Create in me a clean heart, O God, and renew a right spirit
within me.
Psalm 51:10

Being Revived

'It's amazing how a little food can revive you.' This was a thought that came into my mind as we munched into a sandwich as a late tea. We had taken to starting a clear up in the house, which took much longer than usual, and so teatime came and went and it wasn't until 9pm we sat down for something to eat. By then we were all feeling a little worn out, but the sandwich and other food we enjoyed had the desired effect of reviving us and renewing our energies.

Of course, without food, the body weakens, and over a period, permanent damage is done … eventually it will die. It's the same with the soul. Without spiritual nourishment, we become weak inside. And just as we need food to keep us healthy, in energy and vitality, so too we need spiritual food to keep our lives true, pure and pleasing to God. Without it, we become barren, weak and ineffective.

Strange words? Maybe you've never set out on this kind of journey. Maybe never explored all that God has for you as one of his children. You may not even believe … and rob yourself of all God's promises to you. Promises to take care of you, to keep you, to provide the shelter of His love and patience over you, promises to set you free from all that would hinder you.

If you've not really known personally the guiding hand of God in your life, and the reality of His presence with you, then you're invited to the best banquet you'll ever know. God's invitation has your name on it. Come and be filled.

He brought me to the banqueting house, and his banner
over me was love.
Song of Solomon 2:4

Blisters

As a result of playing sport, my younger son finished up with a raw blister on one of his feet, and found that when he went to play some more the following day, the blister was quite painful and effectively meant that he was unable to run much at all.

Fortunately, as you will know, blisters don't tend to stay raw for more than a day or two and so he quickly recovered.

It's amazing that of all the parts in the human body, a very small problem like a blister can effectively bring us to a halt and interfere and put a stop to life. There are lots of similar examples such as a small part not working properly bringing the car to a standstill and so on.

It's true too where our spiritual lives are concerned. A small word spoken out of turn, a lie believed, a moment of foolishness can bring the free flowing of our lives to an abrupt stop, and it feels we can never be the same until whatever it is is sorted. The remedy is to get our eyes back on Jesus. A moment in His Presence and the burden of all the big things in life, as well as the trivial ones, falls off our shoulders to trouble us no more.

Jesus brings rest from all the burdens of life. He specifically promises to restore us. And He keeps His word.

*Restore unto me the joy of thy salvation, and uphold
me with thy free spirit.*
Psalm 51:12

Blocked Drains

When spring is just around the corner, our thoughts turn to the various jobs that may need doing around the house and in the garden, now that we can put our nose out of the front door without the immediate danger of frostbite!

Perhaps you won't thank me for reminding you that the garden will need to be dug over, the lawnmower re-oiled or serviced, the woodwork around the windows stripped down and repainted and so on. Or maybe you are fortunate enough to have someone else to look after these matters for you.

And there's the roof which probably needs to be examined and cleared of moss, leaking gutters repaired and drains unblocked. All these jobs don't need our help to show themselves - they are usually the result of the weather and general wear and tear.

Choked drains seem to me to be one of the worst things that can happen around the house. They quickly upset our daily life and require speedy attention if things are not to get out of hand. It is important that the blockage is removed so that the drains can continue to provide their vital function.

So too with our lives. If we have come to Jesus, asked Him into our lives, and known the joy of His life coming within us, He clears away all things that were in us blocking out His presence and His love.

Yet how quickly our lives can become blocked up again, clogged with the cares and worries of this life, with our wilfulness, our disobedience to God's words to us and our thoughtlessness.

We need to be clear channels of God's Spirit, open to hear and respond to His voice, so our lives are effective for Him and His power is demonstrated within us and through us. It will not happen if our lives are blocking out His Spirit.

Allow Him to keep you clear of all blockages.

Keep thy heart with all diligence, for out of it are the
issues of life.
Proverbs 4:23

Bright Skies Are Always There

Travelling home by car, the clouds were dark and heavy, but suddenly I could see a small break in them, and bright blue sky beyond.

It reminded me that however dark the clouds may be around our lives, God is always faithful and provides a break in them so that they do not overcome us.

But more than that – beyond the darkest cloud imaginable, there is always a cloudless sky. If you have ever been up in an aeroplane as it goes through the clouds to a higher altitude, you'll know what I mean. You come up into bright sunshine all around you. That is such a picture of God – always cloudless skies, always the bright light of His presence … unchangeable, so lovely, so certain, so real.

However dark the clouds are around you, however threatening, however laden with blackness, know that God is there beyond them and just as dark clouds give way to sunshine, so too will the sunshine of His love for you break through and remove the clouds which threaten.

It's the aim of many, perhaps the experience of a much smaller number, to live in that rarefied atmosphere where even the darkest cloud is literally beneath you and not troubling. God calls us to do just that, to live continuously in His presence, to feel His comfort and His solace, to know that whatever our plight, He has been there before us and has triumphed over it.

As I saw the break in the clouds, the certainty of God's promises to me as an individual came into my mind, and I thanked Him for His love and His care for me, and I knew that He would be with me in whatever situations I found myself in the future.

Casting all your care upon him, for he careth for you.
1 Peter 5:7

Bringing Down The Barriers

On holiday, we came upon a great many unmanned railway crossings we needed to get across. They always make me a little nervous, wondering if everyone actually knows where the trains are, and that they are not going to come thundering into you just as you come onto the crossing itself.

Thankfully, we had no problems, and indeed there was only one occasion where the barriers were down and we required to stop and wait.

Barriers, by their very nature, are there to stop you from going ahead, and where level crossings are concerned, they are there for your safety. But there are other kinds of barriers, which prevent us from going forward, spiritual barriers that prevent us from going further in God and from realising all that He has for us.

It may be a bitterness or hurt you have carried around with you all your life or for many, many years, and it effectively stops you from growing in God. It may be a besetting sin, a temptation you collapse at, and can never get past. Or a wilfulness in us where we resist the call of God, not realising what we are doing.

There will be few, if any of us, who have not met barriers in our lives. They can seem unbreakable. Like a horse at a difficult jump, we may have approached them many times, but never got over them. Never been able to clear them out of the way, or find a way through them.

God promises to pull down all the barriers in our lives. Some we will know about, others He will reveal to us. One thing is sure – He will pull them down as we come to Him and ask Him to do so. Take hope – literally nothing is too difficult for Him. He is the Lord God Almighty.

He brought them out of darkness and the shadow of death and
brake their bands in sunder.
Psalm 107:14

Caught In A Frenzy

L ife seems to go at an awful pace for so many people. The days fly by without time to draw breath and with constant rush and pressure. In most forms of business too, it seems that fewer and fewer people are being asked to do more and more work with the danger of increased stress and fatigue. I remember one high flyer even boasting about the fact that he hardly saw his children such was his executive status – has he got his priorities right?

You can even get into the state of mind that there's no time to stop and think, and to survive, you need always to be at a constant state of rush – anything less than that and you begin to feel guilty. It's not true, of course, but feels like it is.

We need time to slow down, to be quiet and at peace. Time to recharge our batteries. Time to be able to take a step back and reflect on what we are doing and why. We need time to nurture ourselves and others around us.

I think Satan, the arch enemy of God, can put a very successful blind-fold around us … to keep us rushing around, here and there, always constantly on the go and worrying about all that we still have to do. If we're in that state we certainly won't have time to stop and listen to what God might be saying to us. How will we hear Him in the hustle and the bustle if He speaks to us in His 'still, small voice'?

There's the challenge. To be able to hear and do all of what God is saying to us. And miss none of it. It will take a steady hand, not one tossed about by rushing around in a mad frenzy of activity.

Thou wilt keep him in perfect peace, whose mind is stayed on
thee: because he trusteth in thee.
Isaiah 26:3

Central Heating

When winter approaches and the days and nights become much colder there can be nothing nicer than returning home out of the cold and feeling the warm blast of heat from inside the house as you open the front door.

We have central heating in our house with time switches to ensure that the house keeps the chill out and is especially warm whenever we want. Even without central heating, a good old-fashioned fire can spread heat and warmth throughout the home, and who amongst us would wish to be without the heat that the fire or the central heating provides?

They spill out soft warmth, heating up the air already there and spreading that warm glow throughout the room and beyond. The cold atmosphere changes to one of warmth where you can feel so much more relaxed and in comfort.

This is a good picture of those of us who are Christ's and have found His warmth, His love and His glow inside us. For they do not remain solely inside us, but spill out to those cold and faint hearts around us, warming their lives with the touch that only Jesus can bring. We are like the fire and the radiators, God's love and care spilling out from us and spreading to those around us, offering change and hope to their lives.

Is it a picture we live up to? You'll know immediately if you do. For you'll be aware both of the warming presence of Jesus in your own life, and of it cascading out and touching those around you.

I have loved thee with an everlasting love: therefore with
lovingkindness have I drawn thee.
Jeremiah 31:3

Change For The Better

Someone, let's call him George, was writing a letter to a long-time friend and mentor who many years ago had exhorted him to a certain course of action, from which he would reap the benefits and achieve much in his life.

Despite the advice of his friend, for whatever reason George had procrastinated, doubting if he could ever achieve that much in his life ... and for many years he had accomplished relatively little when compared to what had been possible.

George suddenly realised that he had not followed the advice of his friend, and the purpose of the letter was to apologise for what had not happened, and also to say that he was now going to do all that he should have done those years ago.

Does this sound like you and God? In the past, has He said certain things to you regarding His Kingdom and your part in it – perhaps issued a call on your life to go and work for Him, but for whatever reason, you never did it?

If so, perhaps the time is now for you to apologise to God for what has not happened in your life, and to tell Him that you are now fully determined to carry out to the letter all He has told you to do.

The calling of God is without repentance. If you are in this position and will take this action, His calling on your life can and will still be outworked. And there may be many who will be in the Kingdom of God, and fed on His Word, because of your actions, however belated they are.

Don't find any more reasons why not to do it – go and get started.

For I have redeemed thee, I have called thee by thy name,
thou art mine.
Isaiah 43:1

Christ And The Commuter

I happened to be in London on business and having arrived there early in the morning after travelling south by overnight train, I found myself joining the morning commuter rush hour to the underground where I had to travel for a few stops to reach my destination.

To say there were a lot of people about would be a grave understatement, as those of you who have travelled by London underground will know. As it happened, the underground train I was on was held up on a few occasions between stations, which gave me a few minutes in the stillness to reflect on my surroundings.

I must say, looking at the people around me, there did not appear to be much cheer about. Many faces carried a frown, possibly due to the delays, or possibly because of some other personal irritation or difficulty. Others seemed to have the load of the world on their shoulders, staring blankly at the floor or windows. Mind you, I myself had a touch of 'flu and probably wasn't a picture of rosiness either!

It did set me thinking, though, that we are very prone to anxiety, fear and discouragement. On returning home I opened the Bible to find that there are many words of encouragement for us.

Lonely? Jesus says: 'I will never leave you, nor forsake you.' Discouraged? The Bible tells us to 'cast your burden on the Lord and He will sustain you.' Weighed down by anxieties? 'Come all of you who are heavy laden, and I will give you rest.'

Ill or depressed? 'He bore our infirmities and carried our diseases.'

Whatever our condition, Jesus has the answer. He has promised to be with us, to guide us and He will show us the eternal secrets of His kingdom. He is the perfect friend who will never let us down.

Fear thou not, for I am with thee: be not dismayed, for I am thy
God. I will strengthen thee, yea I will uphold thee.
Isaiah 41:10

Christmas

S ome friends and I were talking about Christmas and I was reminded by one of them that one of the main aspects of Christmas they love best is the family get-together.

I imagine that for her Christmas has always been a family time, with everyone making a particular point of being together to celebrate the festival, even if it meant long hours travelling in difficult weather conditions.

Families are probably more spread about these days, as ease of travel and mobility of job have taken many of us far away from our parents and grandparents. Nevertheless, it's always good to be together with those you love and to hear again the chuckle and laughter from a favourite uncle or sit and chat with parents, brothers and sisters, grandparents, aunts and uncles. There seem to be so few opportunities these days, with all the bustle and rush of life.

Beyond all these get-togethers, Christmas speaks of one supreme reuniting – that of God and His children. The whole purpose of Jesus' life and death on Calvary was to provide the way whereby we are reunited with our Heavenly Father. If you are still to find Him, He's waiting for you now. No longer the babe in swaddling clothes and lying in a manger, but the One who can change hearts and lives for the better.

And she shall bring forth a son, and thou shalt call his name
Jesus: for he shall save his people from their sins.
Matthew 1:21

Confidence

Confidence. It's probably something most of us don't think about very often, although we will be aware whether we have much ourselves.

And yet it's surprising how often during the course of a week we express our confidence in others. When we post a letter our confidence is that the postal service will deliver it timeously, correctly and in one piece. When we travel by bus, car, or train, we have the confidence to expect that we will arrive at our destination safely. And when we ask a relative, neighbour, or friend to do an errand for us, and they agree to do so, then we have confidence that they will be true to their word.

When we come to the Bible, and the promises of God, we can certainly have the confidence to expect Him to be true to His word. Yet there are Christians who, in practice, don't expect God to fulfil His promises to them. Instead, they live a life of fear and of anxiety, hardly daring to hope that God will help them.

Our lack of confidence can even stem from the fear of fear itself. Not a fear of particular things or anything tangible, just being afraid of having the feeling of being afraid.

Jesus came to set us free from all kinds of fear, and put within us His own confidence. Confidence that defeats the darkest enemy, confidence that fills us with life and with hope.

So if your head is drooping, your eyes only looking downwards, take heart. You can face the future in the strong confidence that God will be faithful to all His promises to you and destroy any fears that you have.

For the Lord shall be thy confidence, and shall keep thy
foot from being taken.
Proverbs 3:26

Connections

Most of our kitchens today have a number of domestic appliances – be it a washing machine, toaster, mixer etc. Over the past 30 to 40 years or so there has come an array of machines to help with the kitchen chores and so relieve us of much of the manual work that our mothers and grandmothers had to do. I well remember as a child the clothes wringer in our house which came to be replaced by an automatic washing machine.

What all these appliances have in common is that they require to be plugged into a supply of electricity before they will work. Without electricity they are useless, but when plugged in and switched on they suddenly come to life and do their job.

I remember a famous preacher who talked about being 'turned on' to Jesus. He explained that his own life had been one of aimlessness and lacking in purpose. But when he found Jesus he found happiness and purpose in life.

With Jesus you find real power. Power to raise the dead, power to heal from all manner of diseases of body, mind and spirit, power to enable us to live above sin and not to fall victim to its temptations.

Check your 'connections'. Make sure they are switched on and there is nothing stopping the flow of God's power in your life. The world today needs Christians to lead effective and powerful lives.

But as many as received him, to them he gave the power to become the sons of God, even to them that believe on his name.
John 1:12

Creepy-Crawlies

I am sure you will remember being at the sea side and turning over some largish stones, then watching all the creepy-crawlies which had made their homes underneath the stone scurry away as fast as they could to the security of another rock.

For exposure of that kind makes them feel afraid and unsafe. And they prefer to live in the dark murky world of the underside of rocks and stones.

When the bright light of God's Holy Spirit shines into a man's or a women's life, our immediate reaction can be to want to do the same as a creepy-crawly does. To run away from that searching bright light and seek cover elsewhere.

For His light immediately shows up all the imperfections that are you and I, and most of us do not want it to reveal all that we are, our ways and our hidden secrets. In practice, God knows them all anyway, but the shining of that light reveals them all too clearly to us as well.

We can run and hide, pretend to ourselves that it didn't happen, or we can turn and 'face the music.' But what is God's purpose in bringing His light in the first place? Is it to condemn us? No. It's to identify to us the impurities that lie within and then remove them so that we can be free of them forever and live out His life in us to the full. After all, it's difficult making sure a pan is spotlessly clean if you do the washing up in a dim light.

If the Holy Spirit is beginning to shine on your life, don't run – it will only be for your good. Stay and watch the miracle God will perform to free you of all that would hinder you in your walk with Him. And know the joy and abounding life which that freedom brings.

Wash me thoroughly from mine iniquity, and cleanse me
from my sin.
Psalm 51:2

'Crucial'

Some years ago, I discovered from one of my sons that 'crucial' was the latest in-word in our part of the world for something really great. Now, in my day, it was 'fab', but it seems we've been through a lot of words since then, 'magic', 'bad', and 'cool' to name a few.

But then everything was 'crucial.' The way he looked, the latest toy, whatever was for tea – it was all 'crucial.' To his father's understanding, all these in the real scale of things aren't crucial at all. But to a little boy's world they were. Of course, we all have our own ideas of what is crucial. 'It's crucial I get to the office on time,' a busy executive might say. 'It's crucial you leave the meat to defrost thoroughly,' your Mum, or the instructions on the packet, might write. 'It's crucial you brush your teeth each day,' says a caring parent.

All of these things may be true, and important. But none of you would believe them to be the most crucial things in life. I wonder how long the list might be, and what it might contain, if I were to ask you to name what you each consider the most crucial aspects of life to be.

The Bible is unequivocal about these matters. 'Except a man/woman be born again,' we read, 'he or she shall not enter the Kingdom of Heaven.' 'For all have sinned and come short of the glory of God,' the Apostle Paul confirms.

Are these things crucial to you? Or have you avoided them throughout most of a lifetime? Or maybe you've never been presented with, or sought out, the facts. Perhaps we will even go to the end of our earthly lives protesting, 'I didn't know – I didn't realise.' Well, God is providing us with the opportunity to know. It's never too late to find out; it's never too late to ask.

For it is time to seek the Lord, till he come and rain
righteousness upon you.
Hosea 10:12

Crying Out Loud

Those of you who have brought up a little baby will know that, apart from being little angels, they can also cry, and cry and cry. Our experience has been no different and all our children had their crying times.

A little one crying out aims to be heard. Whatever the reason for it crying, its objective is certain. 'Come to me – I need you. Help me. Get me out of here – I'm fed up' ... or ... 'I'm hungry' or 'I'm wet!'

And, of course, if our little ones didn't call out, we wouldn't always be aware of their needs, although, where Mums are concerned, they seem to have some in-built knowledge of when baby needs her.

This picture reminded me of some of God's words to us. 'God will deliver the needy, who cry out, the afflicted who have no-one to help,' we read in the book of Psalms. If we don't cry out, then how will God hear of our need? While I believe that God knows all about us already, He encourages us to call out to Him for help, to tell Him we need Him and to seek Him out.

Sometimes we can be in situations that appear to us to be hopeless ones, and there's no one we can turn to. Perhaps you're in just that kind of situation just now, not knowing what to do and feeling unable to share your situation with anyone. Cry out to Him ... the One who loves you so ... the One who can turn the darkest night into day. God will respond to your cry and deliver you from your distress.

Be pleased, O Lord, to deliver me: O Lord make haste to help me.
Psalm 40:13

Day Of Reckoning

Many people do not like the idea of a 'day of reckoning.' It seems to them that the idea of there being consequences for the way they live their lives or for the various actions they take through a lifetime, is an unfair one.

And yet, of course, throughout our lifetime there are many 'days of reckoning' to be encountered. Consider a few examples.

Firstly, the young man learning, say, French at school. To become proficient in learning another language, indeed any subject, study is necessary. But if our young man decides to ignore the studying and pass the time in other pursuits, then his day of reckoning might well be the examination room when he is unable to answer the questions posed.

I suppose all businesses, too, have regular days of reckoning when the calculations are made to see how much profit, or loss, has been realised. Business decisions are also made by individuals – whether to invest in the stock exchange or purchase life assurance might be examples, and they bring their own rewards or lack of them, depending upon what was decided upon. So too the farmer, or market gardener, when sowing his fields in the spring, looks forward to a day of reckoning when he will have sold his full-grown crops, hopefully at a satisfactory return for his endeavours.

Is it really a surprise then, that the Bible also talks about a day of reckoning, when each of us will stand before God to give account of what we have done with our days?

God has given us free will, enabling us to choose our way of living. We can choose to listen to His Word and obey His commandments, or we can choose to go our own way and live as we please. Whichever way we choose has consequences. If we are sowing in our lives seeds of wrong doing, or unrighteousness, should we not expect the consequences to be unfavourable?

And, if we walk according to God's ways, we shall reap the rewards of a life with deep fulfilment, and an eternity with Him.

Let's choose wisely.

So then everyone of us shall give account of himself to God.
Romans 14:12

❧

Deadlines

❧

D eadlines – how most of us hate them at one time or another. They make our lives seem so regulated that we are never a free agent. We feel governed by them – deadlines for getting to work, lunchbreaks, school bells, meetings with clients, for paying bills, for train times or aeroplane and boat departures and so on. And if we miss any of these last examples, we've literally missed the boat and cannot pull the clock backwards to remedy matters.

Indeed, many of us would like to be able to turn the clock backwards and rub out the mistakes we have made in the past, the hurts we might have caused or received, the angry words, the refusal to forgive, our stubbornness and foolishness.

When it comes to a decision to listen to and accept the words of Jesus to us personally, many of us might feel we've missed this particular boat. Perhaps it's because we were quite old and felt past it when we first heard the voice of Jesus speaking to us, or maybe because we've lived the kind of life that makes us feel beyond His help and that Jesus will have nothing to do with us. Or perhaps it's because of a particular difficulty in our make-up, that we feel that we can never be any different.

Well ... there may be many deadlines in life we might miss, but rarely, if ever, while we have breath in our bodies, are we beyond the call of Jesus, or beyond knowing and experiencing His love and His power to save.

I know of many people who thought that they were beyond help, but have found the loving hands of Jesus stretched out towards them and have responded to His call to them. If you've not already come, He is there waiting for you, knowing all about you, arms outstretched to receive you. So, come.

Though he fall, he shall not be utterly cast down: for the Lord upholdeth him with his hand.
Psalm 37:24

❧

Desperation Equals Response
❧

'Desperation equals response' is a little equation I keep in the back of my mind, particularly as I have known its effectiveness on many occasions.

Consider the picture of a young child seeking to attract the attention of his Daddy, who may be engrossed in chatting to a friend about one of his pet subjects. The young child will call to his Dad, but doesn't get any response. So he approaches and stands alongside his Dad, and then right under his nose, but still to no avail. Desperate measures are then taken and, with a measure of risk, the little one gently, then fiercely, tugs at his Dad's jacket or trousers, raising his little voice all the time until Dad just has to notice and deal with all the commotion!

Perhaps sometimes we feel our prayers don't always seem to get a response, or not one we can identify with. Has God become deaf? I don't think so. Has He gone on holiday? Surely not. Then why apparently no answer? Well, perhaps we're just not desperate enough to hear from Him.

In my experience, God answers the prayers of people desperate to get a response. Desperate to see Him move across the face of the earth. Desperate for Him to intervene in some personal way. God loves to hear the prayers of His people and the prayers of a righteous man or woman avail much, we read. So let's get desperate.

Thou shalt call, and I will answer thee.
Job 14:15

&

Eating
&

M ost of us enjoy eating. Certainly I do, particularly if I am a little tired and in need of some energy. There are few people who do not enjoy a good meal, especially when someone else does the preparation of it and clearing up afterwards.

Of course, preparing a meal involves time and effort – buying the basic foodstuffs, often spending hours in the kitchen at the cooker and the sink, and then putting everything into appropriate dishes before it all arrives at the table.

We are usually very careful about what we eat, conscious of the fact that some things are harmful and should not be eaten, and others eaten only after the correct preparation. By eating the correct things our lives are sustained and we are given the energy for the work of the day.

But what about spiritual food? Many of us are not so careful about what we partake of – the things we look at, the books we read, the places we go to.

Jesus is the source of this spiritual food that we need. He said, 'I am the bread of life: he that comes to me shall never hunger and he that believes in me shall never thirst.' He was referring to the 'food' we obtain by walking with Him and partaking of His life - food that will change our own lives, remove the stains from our characters, free us from sin and enable us to grow into His likeness and be effective witnesses for Him. Make sure you get your portion.

Wherefore do ye spend money for that which is not bread? And your labour for that which satisfieth not? Hearken diligently to me, and eat ye that which is good, and let your soul delight itself in fatness.
Isaiah 55:2

❧

Empty Inside
❧

I had to work for a few days during a family week away and returned to our house to collect one or two things I needed.

I was only there for a few minutes when I became distinctly aware of how empty the house felt. Not of furnishings, or the whirring and chanking of kitchen appliances, but of the laughter and shouting of our children, of their thumping up and down the stairs, and the general hubbub that usually goes on in the house. While the house was peaceful, it was empty without these evidences of life.

To anyone else, the house might have looked as it always does, but while perhaps giving the appearance of life within it, it was essentially empty.

It made me think of how empty some of our lives might be. We may give the impression of being full of life, and put on a good face, but deep down inside we are empty, perhaps going through the paces, but lacking real life.

We may even be a Christian, a follower of Jesus, but we are missing the vital ingredient of His power and His love coursing through us.

If so, it's time to find Him. It makes such a huge difference to know Jesus at the centre of your life. You see things so much more clearly, feel His love for you and know His guidance in every aspect of life.

And you're never empty.

Now the God of hope fill you with all joy in believing, that ye may abound in hope, through the power of the Holy Ghost.
Romans 15:13

🐌

Erasing It All

🐌

W hen they were younger, each of our children had a lot of fun with one particular game where you were able to write or draw anything you wanted on a board, using a magnetic pen, and then by pulling a lever across the board, everything you had written or drawn was 'magically' erased and the board was clean and ready for use again.

The principles involved relate to iron filings and the magnetic pen, but they produce a continued sense of wonder at the magic effect of the board being wiped clean at a stroke. Whatever mess we had made of the board, it could be remedied.

That same 'magic' applies to our lives. Each day we are writing the story of our lives. Every item, good or bad, is being recorded as it happens, and at the end of it all, the story that is us, and what we have done with our lives, will be able to be read and displayed.

If the story of your life is a bit of a mess, you're not alone. Sin distorts many of our lives and seeks to destroy us and the potential that is there for us. Sin robs us, robs us of our wholeness and wholesomeness, and tells us that it will never be any different.

I'm sure that many of us would dearly wish we could wipe the slate clean and start again, just as in our children's game board. It is possible.

Jesus came and died to 'wipe our slate clean.' He paid the penalty for all our sinning, which is death. He came to erase all the wrong there has been, and to enable us to start afresh, only this time with His love and His power within us.

Whatever state the story of your life is in, Jesus can change it for the better.

I, even I, am he that blotteth out thy transgressions for mine own sake, and will not remember thy sins.
Isaiah 43:25

Exploration

I remember what we felt like, as children, moving into a detached house in the village where we lived. Until that time we had been brought up in a semi-detached house and while we have fond memories of that house, the move to a detached one is much clearer in my mind.

Suddenly we realised that there were paths which completely surrounded the new building and we were able to run round and round the house while remaining within the garden. Not only that, but the garage was completely detached from the house and also had paths round about it.

To our young minds, our first steps around our new home were like a mystery tour and we spent many days exploring all the different paths and discovering how they joined up with one another.

Now, if I've made this house sound as if it was set in acres of ground, I've misled you. It was an ordinary detached house, a bit bigger than our previous one, but one which to us as small children appeared huge by comparison. It had more rooms as well and it took us some time to examine each room and remember which room was where.

Young children love exploring - indeed I can also remember crawling under the floorboards of a friend's house in amongst all the electric wiring, without a care in the world!

When we come to Jesus Christ and accept His salvation, we need to take time to explore all that is contained within being a Christian.

If my parents had signed the legal documents associated with buying the house I've described, but never moved in, then we would never have had the thrill and excitement of exploring our new house and garden.

And so it is with Jesus. He has opened the door of His house to us, to take us in and provide for all our needs. What are we waiting for? Let us go in and explore all that God has for us.

I applied mine heart to know, and to search, and to seek out
wisdom, and the reason of things.
Ecclesiastes 7:25

Fairy Tales Come True

I was reading a well-known fairy tale to one of my children just before they went off to sleep. For children fairy tales have a magical quality and no matter how often they have heard them before, they love to hear them read over and over again.

In common with most other fairy stories this one started, 'Once upon a time …' and finished, 'They lived happily ever after.' To live 'happily ever after' might seem to be largely restricted to fairy stories these days, with the ever increasing number of marriages that break down, divorces, affairs and so on. Perhaps it's simply an unreal expectation and so has to be reserved for fairy stories. Perhaps we don't work hard enough in our relationships with others to make sure the fairy tale comes true. Or perhaps life throws out obstacles and tragedies that ensure the fairy tale just can't come true.

Yet, consider the story of Jesus in this context. Once upon a time, Jesus, the Son of God in the form of a man, came and lived on earth. He pointed to the way that men and women should live and taught much about life beyond the grave. But there was one huge barrier between man and God called sin, with no way for men and women to overcome it on their own. Then, by taking the judgement and penalty Himself for all our sin and wrongdoing, Jesus unlocked the door for each one of us to be 'born again', to become a new creature in terms of how we live our lives, and thereafter to be with Him in Heaven, and 'live happily ever after.' Not only that, but live with a quality of happiness unsurpassed by anything we have known or could imagine.

It's some offer, isn't it? And yet millions refuse to hear his call, want their own way, and stay outside of His Kingdom. If your life consists of obstacles, barriers, or locked doors that effectively imprison you, Jesus will break them down, unlock you and free you from them all. You'll become an overcomer – you'll be born again and a new person, and what might have, once upon a time, appeared to you as just a fairy tale will become irresistibly real and never fade away.

Ye shall know the truth, and the truth shall make you free.
John 8:32

♣

Feeling Out Of Sorts?

♣

Feeling out of sorts? It's not a happy feeling, is it? You're not feeling yourself, but you can't put your finger on what's wrong, or what's troubling you.

One of my aunts suffered a slight stroke and she described to me the awful feeling she had at the time of being out of control of herself, which was both extremely unpleasant and unnerving. I'm glad to report that she went on to recover, with apparently no long-term effects. She described the experience as a warning to her to take things easier, as a future such stroke might be much more serious or even fatal.

When you're feeling out of sorts, you feel you've no energy for anything. The slightest activity seems to take all the energy you have, and sometimes you don't even want people around you as you've nothing to give.

To be a Christian and to be out of sorts is worse still. For you are no good to anyone where the Kingdom of God is concerned. There are no 'words of life' in you. And if there is unrepented sin in your life, don't expect to feel good. It is vital that our lives are clean before God, if we are to fulfil His purposes as His servants.

If you're feeling out of sorts spiritually, your immediate and only step is to come to God and put matters right. His ear is open to our cry for help and He delights in His children choosing to turn to Him for help.

In my experience it's hard to kid yourself that everything's all right, when it's not. I well remember an occasion many years ago when I was a young Christian and in this condition, one of my friends asked me why I wasn't my usual self ... and I thought I was keeping from all the world that I was feeling out of sorts. I was shocked that it was so obvious.

It's so important that we stay in tune and in touch with God. If you're feeling out of sorts, remedy matters quickly.

And it shall come to pass, when he crieth unto me, that I will hear, for I am gracious.
Exodus 22:27

❧

Fighting The Flab

❧

With my build and shape, I was never likely to become a sprinter, although at school I did quite well in the longer races.

Of course, to become a world class sprinter, or even a local champion, you need to put in an awful lot of hours of hard training. Firm discipline is needed as well as a careful diet and regular workouts. I don't believe there ever has been or ever will be a champion who gets to be one just by thinking about it. It needs action and a lot of it in all kinds of weather, a commitment, a will to succeed and not a little pain and effort.

Many of us may daydream about what we want to be or what it would be like to have this or that kind of success, but it's down to the doing if we are going to make it. And if after a period, we decide to take our foot off the accelerator and lie back for a while, it's sometimes only when we start up again that we realise just how far we have let ourselves go, and that we will need a lot of hard work to get back on track.

Christians too can take their foot off the spiritual pedal with the result that their spiritual muscles go a bit flabby. The realisation comes that we need to sharpen up our commitment and ideas again, and it's then that we find out just how out of shape we have let ourselves get.

For the athlete, it's much harder to get back into shape than it is to keep yourself in shape. As a Christian, it's important that we stay in good spiritual condition as we strive for the prize of the high calling of God. There's no time for sitting back and taking it easy. If we have, let's get back on track.

Study to shew thyself approved unto God, a workman that needeth not be ashamed, rightly dividing the word of truth.
2 Timothy 2:15

❧

Finding The Solid Rock

❧

For some months I watched quite closely the work of a stonemason in our locality. His task had been to repair the front face of an old sandstone building where the stone had become badly eroded by the elements.

What really surprised me was the amount of sandstone he had to hack away with a chisel before he found hard stone, on which he could begin to rebuild the stone's thickness again. This he did by using special screws, which gripped the solid stone, followed by several layers of cement carefully built up until the thickness of the stone returned to its correct level.

'There's no point just brushing off the loose sandstone from the building and then adding new cement' he said 'Before you could turn round, the new coat would have come away from the existing stone. You've got to go back and dig deeply into the stone face until you find solid rock before all the repairs will be effective and stand the test of time.'

How true for you and me too. In the fast changing world of today, we need to have something solid to build our lives upon. Something which will not give in at the first sign of trouble, something that is not a mere fad, here today and gone tomorrow, nor something or someone we go crazy over only to find they let us down.

You've guessed it ... the solid rock is Jesus. He is utterly dependable. He will never let you down, and you can safely build your life upon Him and His words to you. How many are the wrecks of humanity who have ignored Him, and gone their own way, only to find that at the end of the day life held perhaps only pain and loneliness for them.

Make sure you build your life on the solid rock, not shifting sand.

There is none holy as the Lord: for there is none beside thee:
neither is there any rock like our God.
1 Samuel 2:2

Flat On Your Face

S taying with some relations I was out and about to collect the morning newspaper and some rolls. The paper shop was only a short distance away and to reach it I had simply to walk up a slabbed path and thereafter cross the road. Straightforward enough.

However, coming to the end of the path I stubbed my toe on the inside edge of the pavement and, after trying desperately to keep my upright position, I fell flat on my face, falling my full length across the pavement and on to the road. If you have ever done anything similar you will know the thoughts that go through your head trying to avoid falling like that.

Apart from a rather sore toe and some minor cuts to my hands (I managed to get them in front of my face before hitting the ground) I was none the worse for my experience. I continued across the road, bought the newspaper but could not get any rolls and, on returning home, discovered that I had gone to the wrong shop and should have used another one, closer by, which would not have meant taking the route I took.

So, summing up this experience, I was going in the wrong direction and fell flat in my face!

Are you going in the wrong direction? Is your life one that you would be proud of if it was laid out for all to see? Are you pursuing an objective which, deep down, you know is not really right for you, but justified it to yourself on shaky grounds? Or have you heard the voice of God speaking to you about your life and chosen to ignore it? Then expect to fall flat on your face. If your life does not come up to God's standard, don't expect Him to be pleased with you at the end of the day.

So take a look at yourself and see in which direction your life is heading. If it's not Godward, it's time for change.

The eyes of the Lord are in every place, beholding the evil and the good.
Proverbs 15:3

Fool's Gold

I heard once of the large number of people in a certain part of South Africa who rushed to a part of the country where it was understood a seam of gold had been discovered. Hundreds of people arrived with picks, hammers and chisels to try and dig their fortune.

And gold-looking nuggets they found, which only drove them harder in their search and brought more fortune seekers to the area.

The 'gold' was eventually sent for examination and regrettably for all the diggers concerned, analysis confirmed that it was a metal known as 'fool's gold' because of its deceptive colour and feel.

The hopes of wealth were dashed, and all the hard digging and chiselling had been in vain.

Many of us strive throughout our lives to reach whatever goal we think is important, whether it be wealth, or an executive job, possessions or power. We think to ourselves 'If only I had more money, or a better house or a new job, then I would be really happy.' And yet many of those who do in fact reach their self made goals, having arrived, feel, 'Why is there not more to this? Why don't I feel satisfied with my achievement?'

The truth is that no material wealth nor possessions nor power will ever bring that sense of deep satisfaction we are searching for. It does not come from these sources.

Jesus knew this and told his disciples to set their hearts on eternal things. He said, 'Do not store up for yourselves treasures on earth where the moths and rust destroy, and where thieves break in and steal, but store up for yourselves treasures in heaven.'

Have we got our priorities right? Are we more intent in gathering material wealth and possessions than spiritual ones?

Jesus will show us the way to real satisfaction. It comes from knowing Him, putting aside our own endeavours and trusting Him to lead us in our daily lives. He brings new hope, new purpose and happiness beyond comparison.

For where your treasure is, there will your heart be also.
Luke 12:34

Forgiveness

For much of the past 20 years or so I have been involved in what is often called 'customer care' within both large and small businesses, which are encouraged into thinking up ways of beating their customer expectations, and surprising them with added value, or improved service.

If this sounds like a lot of jargon, consider for a moment how you feel when a business goes out of its way to give you the best quality of service they can, and better than you expected. You feel good.

And think about how you feel when people don't act quite as you expect them to, but bring a special kindness and generosity of spirit into your dealings with them. Again, you feel good.

I had the experience of sensing how God deals with sin, and us the sinner. We expect punishment for wrongdoing, harsh words and anger, because this is what we expect another person to dish out to us. Yet when we bring the sin to God and seek His forgiveness, we find an overwhelming sense of His love for us, His forgiveness and His help to stop us sinning again. God hates the sin, but really loves the sinner.

C S Lewis, the famous author, wrote a book called 'Surprised by Joy', and this is just what happens when God touches our lives. I remember so well when one of our young sons declared to us after one Sunday School occasion that he had felt he had been struck by a bolt of joy. It's a feeling not to be missed.

Just as God wants to destroy all the sin in our lives because it pulls us down, He also delights in showering upon us His love, His peace and His forgiveness.

There is joy in the presence of the angels of God over one
sinner that repenteth.
Luke 15:10

Free Offers

W e seem to be inundated, these days, both through the post and by e-mail, with a range of free or discount offers, covering a whole range of goods. Maybe it's because my details are on an ever increasing list of databases used for mailing purposes. Or maybe I am a highly suitable market for these goods, because I own a credit card, or a house or whatever.

Most if not all the offers I have received have a catch to them. Either the goods were not absolutely free, or by taking the free item you commit yourself to buying more in the future at a significant price or you have to pay an 'administration' charge of some kind to be able to take up the 'free' offer. Most of these offers have finished in the bin, with only one or two set aside for consideration.

There are very few things in life that are entirely free. The house we live in, the water we use, the car we drive, the food we eat ... all cost us money, and usually more than we would like. Even the air we breathe costs many of us in terms of our health, because of the impurities the air contains.

When we turn to the Bible, the offers Jesus makes us are truly free. Money has no value for these. We cannot buy ourselves into heaven, just as we cannot buy an extra foot in height.

Jesus' offers include freedom from sin with all its penalties, peace and security, the unsurpassed love of God in our hearts and everlasting life with Him in heaven. If you haven't responded to these offers, now's the time to do so.

Ho, every one that thirsteth, come ye to the waters, and he that hath no money, come ye, buy, and eat, yea, come, buy wine and milk without money and without price.
Isaiah 55:1

Full Of Good Intentions

S ome time ago I moved from a job where I headed up a
department of a large national business, responsible for more
than 50 staff, to a new job in a much smaller organisation
which had begun to expand its size and its activities.

In my former job, many of our responsibilities and workload were
handled by teams of people, depending upon the particular markets
we were involved in. I also had a very able secretary who not only
produced all my reports and correspondence using a personal
computer, but also took care of all my travel arrangements, schedule
of meetings and so on.

In my new role I had to take care of all these things myself, albeit
they were not on the same scale as before, and I learned one lesson
very quickly. This was to deal with matters as they arose, rather
then put them to one side to pass on to another, or to look at when I
had more time ... for there wasn't anyone else at that time to pass
them on to, and I never would have more time later on.

In things Christian, it is always better to take prompt action too.
When God's Holy Spirit speaks to you about a certain matter or to
carry out a commission, do it right away. Don't leave it until ...

And don't say, 'Yes, I'll do it', and then never carry it out. All of
us feel let down if someone promised to do something for us, and
then did nothing about it. Don't be known as one of good intentions
which never come to anything.

God chooses to use us. Let's not let Him down.

The Lord render to every man his righteousness
and his faithfulness.
1 Samuel 26:23

Gathering Riches

I gather that British workers work the largest number of hours per week in Europe; not all of us by desire, I suspect. I am horrified each time I read the number of hours junior doctors have to work, especially as they may well be dealing with life and death issues. My job at least does not directly have that implication.

Stress caused by long hours can be a killer too. Yet many of us plough on hour after hour, night after night, week after week to make more and more money or just to make ends meet, often putting into second place our health, our family and our friends.

There needs to be time too for our spiritual lives. Life is lived at such a pace these days, that many of us hardly have the time to sit down. And we can amass much cash, but we cannot take it with us.

If we are asked at the end of our lives what wealth we have accumulated, some of us may be able to point to the money in our bank accounts and the homes and cars we own. Others will be able to point out the quality of the family they have reared and nursed. But how much will we have amassed in terms of our spiritual lives, the quality of our relationship with Jesus, the depth of His life and His love in us, and the outworking of that love through us to others?

Would you consider that to be 'wealth'? If not, you are unlikely to have met Jesus. For in meeting Him, you will have met an unceasing power of love, and your life will have been enriched beyond your belief. You will have met peace, as you've never known it, and happiness that doesn't come from large bank balances.

For what shall it profit a man, if he gain the whole world,
and lose his own soul?
Mark 8:36

Getting Past The Gift Wrapping

W e were discussing with friends the giving of Christmas and birthday presents to young children. Our friends were asking what would be a suitable present for a one-year-old child. 'Oh', someone responded, 'don't worry about the present. If my children were anything to go by, they will be more interested in the wrapping paper than in the present itself!'

And very often it's true. At that young age, the bright colours of the wrapping paper and its ability to crinkle noisily in tiny hands, makes it very attractive indeed.

Of course, as children grow older, they very quickly realise that the wrapping paper, while in bright and attractive colours, is masking what is inside, and the paper is quickly discarded in their excitement to find out what the present is. At Christmas time in many houses, a collector of opened wrapping paper needs to be a speedy worker!

And so children grow to recognise the relative values of the present compared to the paper. I wonder if the same could be said of us regarding the real values in life.

Perhaps we put all our store in life on the material things our wealth can bring us. Perhaps we are entranced by the allure of the bright lights this world can offer us. Could it be that we are not recognising the value of the promises that Jesus offers, and relatively speaking, still playing with the things of little value? If you've never got past this wrapping paper, ask Jesus to show you in detail the gift inside. It's of priceless value. Jesus Himself died to provide it.

It's changed the life of millions. Comforted the broken hearted, put new power into the faint and weary of heart. Set free those who have been tortured in mind and in spirit. Healed sick bodies and breathed new life into the dying.

It's brought happiness instead of worry. Confidence instead of fear and anxiety. Joy instead of sadness. And faith that grows and grows and grows.

*For the wages of sin is death, but the gift of God is eternal life
through Jesus Christ our Lord.*
Romans 6:23

❧

Getting To Know Him
❧

Walking along a busy street, I passed somebody whom I thought I knew, but I just couldn't put a name to the person, despite racking my brain for sometime afterwards. I'm sure you will have had the same experience.

Each of us will know a large number of people, but to varying degrees. As I walked along the street that day I passed literally hundreds of people whom I didn't know at all, save the one whose face I felt I knew. Then, of course, we have acquaintances we may have been introduced to at some time or other, but we really know little or nothing about them, except that they work for a particular employer, or shop at a particular store.

We may have a significant number of friends, some of whom we will know much better than others. The closest of these we will probably know pretty well – their likes and dislikes, what makes them laugh, their priorities in life and so on.

And then there's our family whom I expect we will know best of all, be it husband or wife, parents and grandparents, brothers or sisters, children or grandchildren. We probably know them intimately, having lived with them for a long time. I know of some people who are aware of what their brother or sister is feeling, even if they are miles apart.

Many of us will go to Church and call ourselves Christians, and yet I wonder how well we know Jesus who is so central to the Christian faith. Is He just a name in a book, a name known to us, but little else? Or could we provide a lot of information about Jesus, but still not know him personally?

Have you met Jesus personally? He is anxious that you do. He is interested in you personally … in all that you are and all that you do.

Grasp the opportunity and get to know Him.

That I may know him, and the power of his resurrection, and the fellowship of his sufferings.
Philippians 3:10

&

God And The Past

&

When looking through some papers in an effort to tidy up a lot of paperwork that had been put to one side over quite a period, I came across some old report cards indicating how well (or not so well) I had done at primary school. Now, I don't intend to go into the details of these reports here, but the discovery of the cards got me reminiscing of school days.

And it also set me thinking that, irrespective of whether the reports were good or bad, one thing was certain, they couldn't be altered now - I couldn't go back to the primary school and set about trying to improve the various marks I received as a youngster.

It's very much like that throughout our lives - we cannot go back and alter the record once it's set - be it school reports, medical history, marriage certificates and so on.

Yet there's little doubt about it - most, if not all of us would very gladly alter some of the records of our lives, but it seems we are saddled with the records as they are.

Or are we? The Bible very clearly talks of new beginnings. No, not going back to earlier days and rewriting the story of our lives, but our past records being put to one side as far as the future is concerned.

When we come to Jesus Christ and ask Him into our lives, He puts our past into 'the sea of God's forgetfulness' as the Bible describes it.

God nullifies the effects of our past. For example, I know of many whom God has healed in a moment of time - changing forever what had gone before. I know of others whose lives were in a mess until God rescued them and changed them so that the circumstances they were in had no further hold over them.

Finding God and inviting Him into our lives is the beginning of a new adventure - one that leads to real and true happiness, because He loves us and cares so much for us.

> *Wherefore he is able to save them to the uttermost that*
> *come unto God by him.*
> *Hebrews 7:25*

God's Wondrous Love

I had an impromptu meeting with a chiropodist when I asked him to take a look at one of my toes which was giving me some discomfort. I'm fortunate enough not to require to visit a chiropodist on a regular basis, but he was visiting and I took the opportunity of an informal consultation.

He looked at the toe and than took my foot pulse, asked whether I have small veins, which I have, and then told me the problem and the solution for it. I was amazed that from such simple actions he could tell what was wrong and how it could be put right, and in particular how my pulse appeared to tell him so much. Clever people, chiropodists.

Often we wonder how, what appears to be a faraway God could possibly know all about us, and then be able to come and sort out all of life's problems with us. But then, that's God, and that's exactly what He does and can do.

But perhaps a bigger wonder is the quality of His love for us. If you've never experienced it yourself, you will not be qualified to comment. Again, we read that if we who are human know how to love and care for our children, how much more will God love and care for us. Many folks I know personally are discovering this for themselves, and it's way, way beyond both their expectations and their imaginations. It's mind-blowing, it's 'out of this world', it's … God.

We will never be able to understand God and all of His ways with us, but we can experience Him for ourselves.

Draw nigh to God, and he will draw nigh to you.
James 4:8

🐘

Go For Gold

🐘

'The good is the enemy of the best.' At first glance, a strange saying, and one I have only heard discussed on a few occasions, but each time it has left an impression on me.

I imagine we are all very thankful when the adjective 'good' is applied to something or someone. Good economic prospects, a good performance at school or at work, a report which indicates that good progress is being made and good behaviour all sound good to hear and rightly so.

But for some, 'good' is not good enough. To become the best in your field, whether it be sporting achievements, or a work situation, you need to be better than good, because there are so many others who are also good at what they do. To reach the pinnacle of success, 'good' will not do. We might settle for a 'good' report or 'good' progress, when we are capable of being one of the best, with the result that we never achieve what is possible for us.

If our heart is set on being one of God's choicest servants, then simply being good, whether in the eyes of the world or of our friends, will not do. We need to set our sights higher and live our lives really close to God, ready to respond and obey His gentlest whisper to us.

If any man serve me, let him follow me.
John 12:26

###

Going Round In Circles

###

W e visited a new, large aquarium on holiday. All of us, particularly the children, gain a lot of pleasure in seeing all the various exotic sea creatures swimming in what closely resembles their natural habitats, and there are some extremely colourful fish and other sea creatures around. The children much enjoy being able to touch some of the other creatures with their hands, and feel the rough and smooth textures of their skins.

At this particular aquarium, there was a new, huge 360 degree tank. Visitors come up into the middle of the area, rather like coming into the hole in a polo mint, and all around you there are various types of fish swimming in a circular motion wherever you look.

It certainly was novel, but I wondered how many of the fish, if any at all, realised that they were simply swimming along in a permanent circle and never getting anywhere at all. It reminds me of the motorist who travelled all day and most of the night round the circular M25 motorway in London, thinking he was travelling to his destination hundreds of miles away!

Always on the go, but never going anywhere. I'm sure some of us feel exactly that way sometimes. Life has a habit of making us feel that way, but it doesn't need to be so. We all have a destination, and an eternal one at that. And we can find the way. Jesus knows it, He knows us, and He will give us the right directions.

If you're swimming along with the crowd, not really knowing what life is all about and where *your* place is in it all, let Jesus show you and reveal Himself to you. He is *the* way.

In all thy ways acknowledge him, and he shall direct thy paths.
Proverbs 3:6

&

Going The Wrong Way

&

I was leading a business acquaintance to and from my office and, at one point, he got ahead of me and, thinking that he knew the way, turned to his left, only to go in the opposite direction to the way he should have gone.

It's an easy mistake to make, particularly if, as he was, you are not familiar with the layout of offices, some of which resemble rabbit warrens in their construction of corridors and rooms. However, if he carried on going the wrong way, he would have finished up completely lost and certainly not at the part of the building he wanted to go to.

It's so easy to go the wrong way, especially if you are not sure of the way. It's true of life itself. We need a guide to keep us on the 'straight and narrow.' Often it is our parents who guide is through our early years so that our values are true, our morals high and our dealings with others fair. Some of us will have parents who have not been good teachers by example, but others of us will be grateful for the love, care and training we received from them.

Jesus said 'I am the vine and you are the branches. Abide in me, and I in you. As a branch cannot bear fruit of itself, except it abides in the vine, neither can you unless you abide in me.' Now, while we don't see many vines in this part of the world, the principles remain true. If we live our lives outside of Christ, we will not live the quality of life and of loving that is there for us. We need to abide in Jesus, to make our home in Him, for there we will find real joy, real peace and real contentment.

Abide in me and I in you.
John 15:4

Going To Battle

Imagine for a minute or two that you are a warrior at war with an enemy. There you are out on the hillside knowing that if you and your army do not kill the enemy, they will kill you. And so you strengthen your resolve and go out to battle.

And go you must, for to stand by and do nothing will mean defeat and slaughter. You must go and fight and you must be full of fire and vigour if you are to be successful.

Now come with me to another scene, another battlefield. You are one of God's children, a Christian by profession of your faith in Jesus and by your conversion, and your enemy is Satan - the fallen angel who hates God and will do anything he can to disrupt and destroy the spiritual life you have inherited in God.

So what do we do? Stand aside and run from the fight? Compromise will mean that our effectiveness for God will be destroyed anyway. We need to stand and fight, not to go home and hide. To go through and face the enemy who will try to destroy our faith and our confidence in God. He'll throw our past at us, our weaknesses and our inabilities. He'll tell us that we will never be of any use to God. But of course he won't tell us the truth that in God we have power over all the power of the enemy.

In these days of darkness, of apostasy, of wickedness beyond belief, of violence, of immorality, of perversion, we who are God's need to stand up and fight. Not to talk about it, but to do it. Let's go out after them, not just stay at home and bemoan how bad things are. Let's go out and count for God.

If God be for us, who can be against us?
Romans 8:31

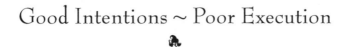

Good Intentions ~ Poor Execution

As a youngster I played a lot of tennis, and I was back on the tennis courts recently, having encouraged my children to have a go. While I managed to get to a reasonable standard as a teenager, a lot of years have passed since then, and I found that I was quite rusty and that a lot of playing and learning would be necessary for me to improve.

I happened to be playing with another of my own age, and we both found that while we knew where we wanted to hit the balls, we were usually unable to carry it off, and the balls often became very wayward! We agreed that it really was a situation where we both had good intentions about directing the ball, but poor execution let us down.

Full of good intentions, but poor in carrying them out, I mused to myself. How similar that is for many Christians. We hear the call of God for our lives, and know the way to take, and intend to carry His instructions out, but for various reasons, our intentions are not fully carried out and so we never reach our full potential in Jesus Christ.

Does that sound a little like you? The great tennis players have to practice, and practice, and practice, as well as listening carefully to, and then carrying out, the instructions of their coaches. Without continued dedication, they won't make the grade.

As Christians we have a wonderful coach in the Holy Spirit, who directs us in the way to go, and if we will heed and carry out His instructions, our lives will be revolutionised. But we need to work at it, being careful to follow His instructions to the letter, being dedicated in our purpose, and confident that He who has called us will bring to fruition all His promises to us.

Don't hold back. Forget the reasons why you can't, and just go for it. If you do, wonderful times lie ahead.

Teach me to do thy will: for thou art my God: thy spirit is good;
lead me into the land of uprightness.
Psalm 143:10

Harmony

I'm sure most of you will enjoy sitting back and listening to the sounds of the world's major orchestras. Almost whatever our choice of music, we can derive a lot of pleasure from listening to all the various instruments combining, under the direction of the conductor, to produce the most beautiful strains and harmonies.

The wide range of instruments in an orchestra can combine in so many different ways to produce wonderful harmonies but, of course, they all need to be in step with the conductor and with each other.

If even one of the instruments is out of tune or out of time, real disaster can follow, the desired harmonies are spoiled and the sweet sounds of the orchestra jarred. The musicians involved are trained professionals who spend considerable time before a performance making sure all their instruments are exactly in tune.

In life, we also speak of being in harmony but, if we were to liken the world to an orchestra, there is so much that is out of tune producing disharmony almost everywhere.

To put it bluntly, mankind is out of tune. We are out of tune with ourselves, with each other, even with nature. We have decided we do not need to stay in line with our fellows, nor with any 'conductor' of our lives.

And so there are discordant notes everywhere. Anger, hatred, jealousies, envies, malice, evil speaking to name a few.

We need to find the one 'conductor' who can make real harmony possible – God Himself. By coming under His direction and obeying His call we will find that all the jarring edges of our lives and our living will be removed and our lives enriched by His Life and His Power.

Beloved, if God so loved us, we ought also to love one another.
1 John 4:11

Headlines

'**W**orldwide, a mother watches her children die of diarrhoea every 8 seconds.' 'Young girl repeatedly raped by gang.' 'Man killed over jacket.' 'Recorded child abuse reaches record proportions.' '12,000 killed in battle to regain town.'

These have been headlines of recent times. Awful, aren't they? The world lurches from crisis to crisis without any apparent ability to stop unspeakable atrocities of every kind. And make no mistake – I have not had to search hard to find these headlines; there have been many other similar ones about.

What's gone wrong? And how does it affect you and me? It's become all too easy to feel that individually none of us can affect what's going on, and we feel impotent to act. I have a quotation on my desk that says that 'the only thing necessary for evil to triumph is for good men and women to do nothing.' It's a fact. If we sit idly by, evil will triumph. Through the centuries, if good men and women had not stood up and been counted, and worked tirelessly for good, there would be much more injustice, few places of physical and mental shelter, fewer hospitals and so on.

'But what can *I* do?' you may ask.

Stand and be counted. Evil doesn't need to triumph – yet often we let it. And pray. Someone said that when he prayed 'coincidences' happened. God answers prayers. His Holy Spirit directs them in us. Spoken and unspoken ones. If you're concerned about the moral state of your street, your town, and your nation – pray as never before.

God will be with us as we stand up for what is right, what is holy, what is good. It's time to take up the challenge.

Stand therefore, having your loins girt about with truth, and
having on the breastplate of righteousness.
Ephesians 6:14

Healing For All

I heard a remarkable story of a man who was miraculously healed as he literally lay on his deathbed. His sister is well known to me, and told me what happened.

The gentleman concerned had suffered a brain haemorrhage and was taken to hospital very seriously ill. His sister was called urgently on the telephone and told that he was not expected to live beyond a few days and if she wished to see him alive, she should make arrangements to visit by the weekend. She did so, but telephoned another relative to ask for members of his church to pray for the individual, which they gladly did.

The sister made arrangements for the long journey and travelled with the intention of setting up the funeral arrangements. When she went in to see him, she had the opportunity to pray at his bedside for his healing. The gentleman was by now in a coma, but she felt a lightening of its intensity as she prayed.

In the time that followed things continued to change. He began to come round and soon was able to speak clearly to her. He was transferred to another hospital but she was told by the doctors not to get her hopes up as he was still bleeding internally and too weak to undergo an operation.

However, the bleeding stopped too, and before long he was able to go home and is now back to his normal health and strength, living alone and fending for himself as previously. The doctors are astounded as they were adamant that he would not live. The truth is that God's healing power was at work.

Thrilling, isn't it? The gentleman concerned is not a Christian and doesn't know Jesus personally at all. But God's love reached out and touched him and made him well.

I am the Lord that healeth thee.
Exodus 15:26

His Love Melts The Hardest Heart

I took to cleaning out our chest freezer. It hadn't been done for a while and quite a bit of ice had built up, which had made the lid difficult to close properly. Armed with scraper (and hammer for the difficult bits), I set about removing all the ice. It took quite a while, and before I had finished, I had amassed three large plastic washing up bowls full of ice.

The mountain of ice looked a little daunting, and much of it was hard as nails, and would not break up at all by hand. But, as you and I both know, there is an easy way of dealing with ice … and into the sink it went. The hot water soon made little of it all, and allowed me to pull out the drowned peas, sprouts and the occasional potato fritter that had escaped out of their packets.

Heat and warmth have the marvellous ability to break up fast the hardest piece of ice, and the love of God can break down the hardest heart. I don't care whether you're a hardened alcoholic or drug addict, whether you are the bitterest person alive, if you will let the love of Jesus touch you for a moment, He will take all that hardness away, and replace it with the warmth and happiness of His love and His joy inside you. When was the last time you felt that sudden, deep welling up of joy in your heart, for no apparent reason?

A hardened alcoholic I know found that Jesus could take all his need for alcohol away and replace it with something much better. And his family life, which had been destroyed by his drinking, has been restored. His friends and colleagues say they are now the perfect family, and the family are out and about telling others of how the love and forgiveness of Jesus have changed them all.

Nor height, nor depth, nor any other creature, shall be able to separate us from the love of God, which is in Christ Jesus our Lord.
Romans 8:39

Holy Excitement

Some people take the view that you shouldn't get too excited about Christianity or about being a Christian. How strange that is!

If you've ever been saved from likely death, for example from drowning, rescued from a cliff face, or from a car accident, you are very grateful to the person or people who were responsible for saving you.

There was the case in the Bible of the young man who, wanting his own way, left home for the bright lights in search of the fast life. He eventually came to his senses, having lost all his money and his friends with it, and returned home, to find the welcoming arms of his father. It's a picture of the rejoicing in heaven over every one of us who returns to our heavenly Father.

Now, is it realistic to suggest to a football supporter that he should remain quiet and expressionless when his team scores a vital goal in a league or cup match? I think not. Then why should the Christian who has found the greatest experience known to man be expected not to shout about it and want to tell everyone what's happened to them?

Christianity is vibrant, alive, and deeply satisfying. You're in touch with an awesome and holy God, but also One who loves you and wants you to delight in being His. In the Old Testament David danced and sang before the Lord, and the children of God shouted and sang praises to Him. On many other occasions they were prostrate, down on their faces, before Him. Why should it be any different today?

As God touches our land with His power, and revives its people, expect change. Expect men and women, boys and girls to feel His touch on their lives. Expect conviction for all sin against God and against others. Expect tears of repentance and expect outstanding joy and power as God's forgiveness and His peace are found.

The Lord is my strength and my shield; my heart trusted in him,
and I am helped: therefore my heart greatly rejoiceth; and with
my song will I praise him.
Psalm 28:7

&

Hope

&

I have the feeling that many of us have found that life makes us a little cynical about realising our dreams. Life teaches us that dreams are just that – nice ideas or romantic notions that regrettably never come about in practice. Yes, well, there may be exceptions, but we are not amongst these exceptions.

All too easily, harsh reality catches up with us and overtakes our dreams, squashing them out. And there can come a feeling of never being able to realise our goals, never to experience what we reach out for in our dreams.

I guess it was like that for the disciples of Jesus. They had hoped for so much from Jesus, and there he was, hanging, crucified on a tree with all the hopes and ambitions of His followers apparently dashed and gone forever. Hope had evaporated, despite what Jesus had already told them about the cross.

But Jesus was different and He was the difference. He could, and did, turn things on their head. He was able to make the dream come true. And how many have been changed by that difference – from the dying thief beside Him on the cross who found paradise to the countless numbers healed of all manner of diseases and the millions and millions of men and women whose hearts He has opened up and changed forever, replacing hate with love, pride with humility, anger with grace.

That's how Jesus will change you, too. He will remove the stony heart from you, He will replace despair with joy, fear and anxiety with peace, weakness with strength. You will know how it is to be really loved. And how to love.

Is this all a pipe dream too? I think not. The Bible says not. And countless men and women, young and old, who were once as perhaps you are now, have proved not.

Now the God of hope fill you with all joy and peace in believing,
that ye may abound in hope.
Romans 15:13

❦

How Do You Measure Up?

❦

Attached to one of the inside doors in our house hangs a children's growth chart; the kind of thing some banks and building societies give away when you open a savings account for a child.

From time to time, the children stood in front of the chart, with shoes off and heads straight so that we could measure, and they could know how much they had grown since the last time they were measured. It was marks on the wardrobe when I was young!

Now it wouldn't have been wise for us to try to measure them every day or every week as little change would have been seen. However, by doing it every so often, their progress and rate of growth could be seen and charted.

It's obviously important that our children grow at a steady rate, even if that puts a strain on the budget for both food and clothing! And, in our walk with God, it's also so very important that we grow and progress. Just as we would not wish any child's growth to be stunted, God does not wish that our spiritual lives become stunted either.

How do we measure up? Indeed, how do we chart our progress? It would be of value to each one of us if, every so often, we stopped and took a long hard look at ourselves and our relationship with God.

God never leaves us in the dark on these matters – it is the Holy Spirit's desire that we should grow into the likeness of Christ and He is there to enable us to do so.

I press toward the mark for the prize of the high calling in Christ Jesus.
Philippians 3:14

&

Hungry For God
&

I don't suppose many of us have really known what it is to be desperately hungry for long periods of time, although there have been, and continue to be, hard times for some. Certainly the younger ones of us in Britain have only known shops and supermarkets stacked full of all kinds of foods, and if we do get hungry, a trip to the kitchen soon fixes that.

But there remain so many parts of the world where hunger, and acute hunger at that, is a way of life. Where not only is the next meal not in the larder, but there is no knowledge where it will come from. Imagine that you are in one of these parts of the world; you are hungry … extremely hungry, and there is literally no food for miles around. Thoughts of all other matters have long disappeared as you start out again in the search for food. You leave your family and your village to journey for perhaps many, many miles where you have learned there may be some grain available.

Hunger pains drive you frantic in your search for survival for you and your family.

It sounds very disturbing, doesn't it? Yet it's tragically true. There is more than enough food in the world for all of us, but it's not in the right places. Why should people be put in such a desperate plight?

And is this the kind of desperation we find ourselves in to know God? Does that sound far too fanatical? The truth is that those who desperately seek to know God find him in great depth, and those who are not desperate probably do not.

As you ask yourself what is the strength of your desire for God, remind yourself of those who go absolutely all out for one earthly meal.

Blessed are they which do hunger and thirst after righteousness:
for they shall be filled.
Matthew 5:6

Illness

U nhappily, every day of the year some of us are taken ill; mostly with a minor ailment, but some are more seriously ill and may require urgent medication or surgery.

If we are the one who is ill, we will want our disease to be correctly diagnosed and, as a result of our doctor's verdict and advice, receive the correct treatment to cure or alleviate our particular ailment.

Imagine you are suffering from a potentially serious affliction in some part of your body. Having been to a doctor, you would not thank him, or think much of him, if he showed little interest in you and just said: 'There, there, there's nothing much wrong with you,' and, sticking a piece of plaster on your skin, said good-bye, turning to see his next patient.

You would thank a doctor who, correctly diagnosing your disease, promptly took action so that you received immediate treatment or surgery. Quite possibly this will involve some suffering and pain, but your life will be saved and you will come forth in due course a healed person.

There are, unhappily, many religious leaders who like a poor doctor brush our condition under the carpet, and give a false assurance to their listeners that there's not much the matter with them and there is no need for alarm or action.

But God and His Word are not like false shepherds. Sin is an evil growth within us and if it is not dealt with, we shall die spiritually. We cannot treat ourselves – patching up leads to failure. The only master surgeon is Jesus Christ.

He knows all about our troubles, and He can deal with them. That is why Jesus came. Only He can make us whole.

For she said, If I may touch but his clothes, I shall be whole.
Mark 5:28

Inheritance

Have you ever been fortunate enough to benefit from an inheritance? If you have, you will probably remember receiving some form of notification of the fact, perhaps by word of mouth or by letter inviting you to be at an appointed place at a given time. On your arrival, the details of your inheritance are given to you.

The whereabouts of some inheritors may not be known, and you may have come across a notice in a newspaper indicating that if the person named makes contact with a certain firm of solicitors, he or she 'may learn something to their advantage.'

Given news of an inheritance, most of us will not waste much time in making suitable arrangements to attend the place appointed. There will be few of us who will say, 'An inheritance – so what! Maybe I'll go – then again, maybe I won't,' and act very casually about the matter. No, we make sure we are able to attend to find out what our inheritance is.

Well, I have good news for all of us – there is an inheritance for each one of us about which we have already been notified!

What is this inheritance? Victory over sin, freedom from fear, and a love for others we never dreamed we might have - these are just some of the elements included. Above all, it includes the certainty of everlasting life with Jesus Himself.

As with some other inheritances, there are conditions attached. We need to repent of our wrongdoing and ask Jesus to come and live in us. Repentance is not a fashionable word nowadays. It involves an acknowledgement of our weakness and humility to ask for forgiveness. But having fulfilled the conditions, this inheritance surpasses any other we could wish for.

But my God shall supply all your need according to his riches
in glory by Christ Jesus.
Philippians 4:19

❧

Knowing The Rules

❧

One of my young sons was trying out a new game on a personal computer and was not readily understanding how the game was played, and what he should do to win. After watching what was happening when he pressed various keys, he was not much the wiser and so asked me what the game was all about.

I suggested we look up the instructions and having clicked on the appropriate keys, they were displayed on the screen and we learned the objectives of the games and the scoring system etc. Then, before long, instead of losing all the games, he got the better of his computerised opponents and went on to win every game he played.

Funny that, isn't it? You can go about in the dark for ages, but when you know the rules and how to play, everything changes and you can become a winner.

The same principles hold true for life. We can go on through much, if not all, of a lifetime, in the dark so to speak, about what life is all about, what the rules are, and about what we need to know about it all.

Yet we have a rulebook readily available, certainly in this part of the world. The Bible tells us clearly about life on earth, about ourselves, and about what we need to do to have eternal life with Jesus, and about eternal death in hell without him. Yet many of us never get to grips with the rules, and so we can expect to stay in the dark and never realise our destiny, and at the end of it all, find eternal night.

We probably feel that a person would be quite foolish to try and play a game without understanding the rules, yet do we do the same as far as the things of God are concerned? Surely something as major as our eternal destiny is worth finding out about before we go much further?

Let God's Holy Spirit move you towards the truth and claims of Jesus, and discover your real purpose of living.

For God so loved the world that he gave his only begotten Son, that whosoever believeth in him should not perish, but have everlasting life.
John 3:16

Light And Darkness

W e had one of the first glimpses of spring sunshine streaming through our office windows, and it was lovely to have the warmth of that spring brightness bursting in upon us, but it also highlighted very clearly how dirty our windows had become.

Though they are regularly washed, we hadn't noticed just how much dirt they had collected – it was only with bright sunshine upon them and through them that the truth became apparent for all to see. Without that light, we could have gone on a long time assuming they were really quite clean, but in fact, action was required.

When the light of God's Holy Spirit shines, maybe for the first time, on our lives, the same thing happens. As that bright light shines upon us in all its purity and clarity, it shows up all the impurities we have. The wrong way we think, the way we judge ill of others, our liking for what we know is, or could be, wrong and unclean. Indeed, often we don't look a pretty sight.

Is it simply to condemn us? No – God wants His purity and His holiness and wholeness in our lives. He wants them to be untarnished by sin. So the light of the Holy Spirit shows up all that's not clean that He might change our ways, and wash us clean. His objective is that God's light and life should shine out from us - to Himself and to others around us. Not an abstract thought but reality in practice.

Our office windows need to be washed again and again, to remove all the grime and dirt that settles on them. And our lives, too, regularly need to be cleansed of all the sin and impurities that seek to cling to us. God does just that for us as we come to Him.

Thy word is a lamp unto my feet, and a light unto my path.
Psalm 119:105

Little Things Lead To Big Things

I am not an avid decorator but the time arrived when our children's bedrooms required to be redecorated. So my wife and I got our decorating tools together and started the job of stripping off the previous wallpaper.

Now there is an art to stripping wallpaper and, on this occasion, we chose to remove the outer layer of the previous paper, while aiming to leave the lining paper still on the walls, so it required a delicate hand. And for me, there was a real feeling of success, when, having managed to scratch back the tiniest piece of the wallpaper by gently pulling at it the piece I was removing grew larger and larger until a large part of the whole strip had been removed.

'What large pieces can be removed from such small beginnings' I thought. And as I continued, I thought of the many things in life that start out from the tiny beginnings. Millionaires have told how they started with only a pound or two. Many large corporations started life as a small back street shop, office or factory. And in nature too, a vast harvest can be reaped from a small number of seeds.

And this is also true where the Kingdom of God is concerned. Jesus said, 'Where two or three are gathered in my Name, I will be in the midst of them.' And I know of many works of God, now with very large numbers of Christians, which grew out of literally two or three gathered together in His Name.

So, if what you are doing for God seems so small and insignificant – take heart. God is faithful and will nurture the work that He has put in to your hands, as you obey His leading and look to Him to fulfil His Word in you.

Great is thy faithfulness.
Lamentations 3:23

Listening

How many of us are good listeners? I know that there is a real shortage today of people who will take time to listen to the problem of others, and so help them to unburden themselves.

I have taken part in many business meetings, only to find that some of those present spent more time thinking of what they were going to say than they did listening to the others' points of view. It is irritating, isn't it, to find yourself being interrupted by others who don't allow you to finish and by their own statements indicate that they haven't really been listening to you anyway.

It can also be difficult to listen very carefully to someone when you're having to compete with the television or radio, or others in the room drowning out what is being said. I remember on one occasion being invited to someone's house only to find that they kept the television on and tried to keep an eye on what was happening on the TV while endeavouring keep track of what we were talking about!

Many of us may spend a lot of our time listening to and watching what is being said on television, even if it is only some soap opera or other. But how much attention do we give to the more important issues of life and how much listening do we do, where the things of God are concerned? Can we recognise His Voice when He speaks to us?

We certainly won't hear what God is saying to us while our minds and ears are 'clogged up' with the events of the day or the clamouring of the television set. We need to take time to listen to Him. For matters about which He speaks vitally concern each one of us.

There is no voice more worth listening to.

Now therefore hearken thou unto the voice of
the words of the Lord.
1 Samuel 15:1

Listening To God

꩜

I'm sure many of you Mums and Dads will have gone through lots of frustrating times trying to attract the attention of your children for one thing or another, only to find that they are so engrossed in what they are doing that they genuinely don't hear you.

It's maybe the television that's to blame, or maybe they're involved in a game with their pals, or reading some desperately important story in their latest comic - anyway it can seem to take an age to get their attention and a response to your request.

On the other hand, maybe they've decided that it's more convenient to ignore your calls until they hear you get to the point of desperation, or anger, or both. Then it's 'in a minute Mum' or 'just let me finish this story Dad' or other such cries.

And if their delay results in their missing the bus, or their friends, then, of course, it's Mum or Dad that's to blame. 'Why didn't you call me earlier?' they cry, as if we Mums and Dads had been calmly letting the required time to miss the bus elapse.

Now, all this might sound quite amusing, but I, and countless others, know it's not! And thinking about it set me wondering if we, as adults, do the same to God.

God can speak to us on many occasions about His Kingdom and our relationship, or lack of it, with Himself. But we can be too engrossed in what we are doing at these times and, even if we recognise His voice, we say ,'Yes, OK, I'll deal with these issues at another time when it's more convenient,' and so put matters off.

Perhaps we're so engrossed we don't even hear the Voice that is calling out to us. We can go through a lifetime like this, and then when we come face to face with Him on Judgement Day we might cry, 'But why didn't someone tell me about life and death and eternity?' and find the response being 'I did, but you were too busy to hear.'

Hear counsel, and receive instruction, that thou mayest
be wise in thy latter end.
Proverbs 19:20

❧

Looking For Something And Finding The Answer Right Under Your Nose

❧

The name 'Fleur de lys' came into our household as our young daughter was asked as part of homework to draw a picture of it. While we had heard the term before, and knew that fleur meant flower, we couldn't put our finger on it, and so resorted to encyclopaedia and dictionaries, but without success. Even our CD Rom encyclopaedia couldn't come up with the answer.

In the midst of this, one of our sons telephoned a friend and then went over to visit him, and it was from there that the answer came. His friend had a scout belt and the insignia on the buckle was a fleur de lys.

Our son came back triumphantly with the belt to show us all, and then it dawned on us ... that very design was everywhere on our hall carpet, right in front of our noses! We simply had known the pattern by a different name.

It's funny how sometimes you can search and search for something, only to discover that the answer lies right under your nose, or straight in front of you. I reckon that many of us go through life searching for answers to many things, why we are here, what life is all about, how we can find peace and so on. And, you know, again the answer is right in front of us.

In the Bible you'll find the answers to all that life holds for you. Promises from God about His love, His peace, about forgiveness, about change for the better, and about eternal life. God's Holy Spirit will guide you towards Jesus Himself, who will draw near to you and touch your life.

Life's answers are so much nearer than we think. We just don't go looking in the right places for them.

Call unto me, and I will answer thee, and shew thee great and mighty things, which thou knowest not.
Jeremiah 33:3

❧

Lose Your Chains

❧

A headline commentary in a leading business magazine was 'Lose your Chains.' The article was all about competitiveness in business but the thought that struck me in reading the headline was something quite different.

While probably none of us these days has ever literally been or is likely to be in chains, nevertheless for many of us there are issues that effectively make us feel that we are chained down. It might be something in our past that continues to haunt us, it might be physical circumstances that prevent us from being what we want to be, or it might be some besetting sin that has made us a prisoner to it and we feel we can never be free from the sin itself or the guilt we feel because of it.

Here's the good news! Just as the Apostle Paul and Silas were literally freed from their chains in jail, we can also be freed, often instantaneously, from all of the chains that keep us or get us down.

In Jesus there is all authority and a word from Him can literally set us free. Indeed, He came to specifically set us free from all that is wrong in our lives and all that comes seeking to lead astray.

With Jesus, there is perfect liberty. Those who have known His touch and authority in their lives will testify to the complete freedom they have found as they have been delivered from all that has enchained them.

Freedom from fear, for example, is a wonderful inheritance that Jesus offers. There will virtually be none of us who can truthfully say that they have never been afraid. Indeed, some of us are afraid about being afraid.

People from many nations these days cry out for freedom – it can be yours, now.

He brought me out of an horrible pit, out of the miry clay, and set my feet upon a rock, and established my goings.
Psalm 40:2

🐾

Lost ... And Found

🐾

No-one likes to be lost. It can be both a frightening and unnerving experience, particularly if you're young and less able to seek out help. If you're lost, the thought of never being found or never finding the way out can be very real, with the feeling of being lost forever filling us with fear.

A friend tells the story of being lost while out in the car. I'm not sure why he had got himself lost but he was, and he spotted someone at the roadside and quickly stopped alongside. 'Do you know the way to so and so?' he asked, naming the destination. The man replied,

'I do and, more than that, I'm going there myself,' 'Well, if you would accept a lift, I'd be very grateful and perhaps you would give me directions as we go,' my friend replied. 'I'd be glad to,' the man said and in he got.

What were previously unknown hills and valleys, streets and buildings now became clear signposts and my friend was quickly and easily able to be guided to his destination without any hesitation or further wondering whether he was on the right road.

It's rather like that where Christianity is concerned. All of us are travelling along our own particular life's journey and many of us are really quite lost. Worse than that, we can have been misguided along the road and find ourselves quite badly off course.

In our lost state stands Jesus alongside us; Jesus knows exactly what life is all about and all about our particular life … its past, its present and its destiny. We can invite Him to come and travel with us, knowing that He will guide and direct us to eternal life beyond the grave and all the while sharing His life and His power with us.

Or we can refuse His offer of help and go our way with no certainty of finding our way successfully. Let Jesus be your guide. Let Him direct your life. Don't be lost.

For the Son of man is come to save that which was lost.
Matthew 18:11

Love And Sacrifice

Maybe you've heard the true story of an elderly man in China whose car had broken down in the countryside and he had to leave it to go and seek assistance. He walked over the fields and came to a house, the occupants of which were

Christians who invited the man to accompany them to hear a Christian evangelist in another town, which he did.

Over 40 years previously, the man had been severely persecuted for his Christian faith, to the extent that he had been flung into jail for many years. At that time he was bringing up a young son, and with no-one to look after the child while he was in jail, he went to his persecutor and asked him to bring up the child as his own. He had never seen the child since and had heard that he had died.

When the evangelist started to speak, the elderly man recognised the same voice, intonations and mannerisms he knew so well as his own. He discovered that the evangelist was his son, who was not dead as his father had understood. The persecutor had been so taken with the man's sacrifice in asking him to bring up his child that he himself had become a Christian and had brought up the child in the Christian way. Father and son were re-united after 42 years.

There is usually sacrifice in love. And there is usually sacrifice in loving your enemies, as Jesus commanded.

But I say unto you which hear, love your enemies, do good to them which hate you.
Luke 6:27

Love At Christmas*

W e were the only family with children in the restaurant. I sat Michael in a high chair - everyone was quietly eating and talking. Suddenly Michael squealed with glee and said, 'Hi, there,' and pounded his baby hands on the high chair tray.

I looked around and saw the source of his merriment. It was a man with a tattered rag of a coat; dirty, greasy and worn. His trousers were baggy and his toes poked out of his would-be shoes. His shirt was dirty and his hair was uncombed and unwashed. We were too far away from him to smell, but I was sure he would smell.

His hands waved and flapped on loose wrists. 'Hi, there, baby; hi, there big boy,' he said to Michael. My husband and I exchanged looks. 'What do we do?' Michael continued to laugh and answer, 'Hi, hi there.'

Our meal came and the man continued to shout across the room, 'Hi there. Look he knows peek-a-boo.' He was obviously drunk. My husband and I were embarrassed; we ate in silence, except for Michael who was running through his repertoire for this admiring old man.

We finished our meal. The old man was sat between us and the door and as we drew closer to him, Michael leaned over my arm and propelled himself from my arms to the man's in an act of total trust, love and submission. The old man's eyes closed and I saw tears hover beneath his lashes. He rocked and cradled Michael then returning him to me said, 'God bless you, you've given me my Christmas gift.'

I had just witnessed Christ's love shown through the innocence of a tiny child who made no judgement. He saw a soul, while I saw a suit of dirty clothes. I was the one who was blind holding a child who was not. I felt God ask, 'Will you not share your son for a moment, when I am sharing mine for all eternity?'

* *Source unknown*

And to know the love of Christ, which passeth knowledge, that ye might be filled with all the fullness of God.
Ephesians 3:19

Love Never Fails

Love is an extremely powerful force. It breaks down barriers that nothing else can, it destroys insecurity and fears, and can bring such a feeling of well being into our lives.

The love of God for each of us is indescribable. It beggars belief. It can move all the mountains in our lives, it changes all our perspectives, and is such a re-invigorating energy. Everything changes. You never feel the same again. If you have known the love of God gushing through you, you will know what I mean.

You can imagine therefore that, if this force is operating in our lives, we will affect those around us. They will feel the touch of God's love through us and be radically changed themselves.

God tells us that we must love each other. To love the unloved and the unlovely. If you follow the life of Jesus in the New Testament, you will find that he was so often to be found in the company of those whom society had no time for or who were considered outcasts. There are so many today, young and old, who feel unloved, uncared for, and as a result their lives are damaged, and they seek to find happiness in all the wrong places, and by doing all the wrong things.

'But how do I love them? I feel I have no love to give them.' That's probably just as well as our love would be only as strong as we are ourselves. God's love goes way beyond what we as individuals can give. The answer is to open ourselves to receive the love of God within us, so that it can pass through us to those around us so deprived of love for so many reasons.

This is my commandment, that you love one another,
as I have loved you.
John 15:12

Mistakes

I was at my computer screen, looking at some computer accounting data when I noticed a spelling mistake in one of the entries. Being a stickler for detail, which has come from many years' experience proof reading leaflets and brochures, I had to fix the mistake.

This involved changing the screen I was looking at, which then required the program to go back through the accounts to the base entry and change it. Once changed there, all other references to be entered were automatically adjusted, so the mistake was eradicated altogether.

It reminded me of sin, and what Jesus does about it. Many of us tend to cover over our little sins, never mind the big ones, so they don't show, or we hope they won't. Jesus wants to go back to the problem that caused the sin, and to deal with that problem, so that once it is sorted, it won't appear again.

Just as a gardener would like to get all the roots of a weed out of his soil or lawn, so Jesus wants to get to the roots of our sinning, and deal with them. He does not want us to suffer the problem through a lifetime, hampering us and keeping us less effective for Him than we should be.

If you have areas in your life that need dealt with, besetting sins as the Bible puts it, let Jesus probe out the cause of the problem. You'll be free of them forever. Don't paper over them, in the hope that He'll not notice, and then have to carry them around with you like a weight on your shoulders, perhaps through the whole of a lifetime.

We all make mistakes, little ones and big ones. Jesus is the Master fixer.

He will deliver his soul from going into the pit, and his
life shall see the light.
Job 33:28

No Man's Land

No-one likes to be in 'no-man's land.' It's a term which was often used in war situations to describe the ground between opposing enemies and, if you are caught there, you're caught in the middle and not recognised to be part of either side – therefore likely to be attacked by both. So it's hardly a safe place to be.

The term 'being in no-man's land' can also be applied to ourselves. Perhaps we're one of those who, having heard the claims of Jesus Christ on our lives, have responded and asked Him to come in and take control.

And then, as He begins to fulfil His promises to transform us and make us like Himself, we begin to back away, fearful of what the cost might be and of the consequences of our commitment to Him.

So we don't 'burn our bridges' but leave a back door open which we begin to use to retreat from His gaze as our life comes under His microscope. And eventually, often sooner rather than later, we find ourselves in 'no-man's land.' While professing our Christianity and our loyalty to Jesus, we don't practise what we profess but keep our distance from His workings within us.

It's not a happy place to be in, with one foot in Christ's Kingdom and the other firmly rooted in this life.

No man can serve two masters. For either he will hate the one and love the other, or he will be devoted to the one and despise the other. Are we like that? Does our Christianity have many back doors? Or have we given a blank cheque to Jesus to do as He would with us? It's only when a commitment is full that we will realise the benefits of being a child of God.

A double minded man is unstable in all his ways.
James 1:8

Nothing Is Impossible With God

A number of sayings have come into our language over the years, and a new one to me was uttered by one of my friends who said to another, 'Never say never.' Many of you will have heard these words before but the truth behind them struck me anew. In many areas of life we are quick to say that this or that can never happen and sometimes, as a result, our sights are lowered and we commit ourselves to a quality of life that never aspires to what just might be.

This can also be true where our Christian living is concerned. The truth is that nothing is impossible with God but we are prone to limit His sights to the level of our own, rather than look beyond ourselves to what He has planned for us. God is a God of the infinite and he longs for us to leave the realm of the finite.

We read in the Bible that 'if any man is in Christ, he has become a new creature' and as part of this, no longer are we restricted to what our human minds tell us is the way things are, but we are lifted into the supernatural where God's Holy Spirit reveals Christ to us and the way of the miraculous seeks to become the norm.

Everything is possible with God. I know people whose lives have been transformed, where hurts of many years, standing have gone; people healed from illness and pain and those whose character and personality have taken on the qualities of Christ – of goodness, tenderness, and love for others.

So if you are looking for God to do great things in your life, and to make His presence known to you, set your sights high. God's horizons are unlimited. Don't limit them by one iota.

With God, all things are possible.
Matthew 10:26

Not Your Way But My Way

I t's funny how often we think we are right, only to find out later we've got it wrong. It can be quite amusing sometimes to listen to two people battling it out, each convinced that they're right and not giving an inch to the other, even if they're not that sure of their facts.

It seems to be in us to want to beat our chests and pontificate on this point or that, even on the most trivial matters. And when it comes to the things of God you'll hear a whole load of opinions about the meaning of this part of the Bible or of that parable of Jesus.

In life too we want to choose our own way, to do our own thing, and to be able to decide for ourselves what is right and what is wrong. The trouble is that almost always we'll get it wrong. And the worst part is often admitting it.

There is a little verse in the Bible where God indicates that His ways are not our ways and our ways are not His ways, and another where He says, 'There is a way that seemeth right to a man, but the ends thereof are the ways of death.'

God is looking for us to put our lives into His hands and allow Him to lead us in choosing the right ways and making the right decisions in our lives. Left to our own devices we will make a mess of things and yet God promises that with His Spirit within us, we shall have life with a capital 'L.' He promises peace instead of anguish, joy instead of sadness and despair and hope instead of defeat.

Are you ready to admit that you could use a bit of help in running your life? Or are you still saying that you can make a better job of it on your own? Give Jesus a chance to prove to you the difference He can make. You'll be astonished at the changes.

And they'll all be for the better.

For my thoughts are not your thoughts, neither are your ways
my ways, saith the Lord.
Isaiah 55:8

Only Tenants Here

O nly a short distance from my mother-in-law's last but one house is an old folks' home and I had been in the habit of waving to one of the residents I knew there each time we visited my mother-in-law.

The resident I knew died some months later, and the empty window reminded me of her and of her death.

I imagined the room would soon have had a new resident, and the thought struck me that, while on earth, we are merely tenants of all we own, particularly of where we live, and our passing simply transfers the tenancy to another. We all are familiar with the saying 'you can't take it with you,' and indeed you cannot.

We are earth travellers, with our time here only part of a lifetime, if you will hear the Word of God in the Bible.

I wonder what kind of baggage we will actually take with us in our passing? It could well include a memory of all we had done and hadn't done. Most of us may not be too happy about that, particularly if it comes before God himself. It will also include the answers to the question 'What did you do about the claims of Jesus? Did you respond and follow Him? Or did you reject Him and follow your own way?'

Our response to the claims of Jesus will be the ticket to our destination after life on earth. Be not confused, there is a Heaven and there is a Hell and we choose our destination by our response – if you're a doubter, there is plenty of evidence in front of you of those who, while on earth, are in a 'living hell.' But then, if we on earth have followed Christ, our life will have spoken of His love, His life and His power in us. And Heaven will be the most desirable place conceivable – for there we will be with Christ forever.

Tenants here – but where will be our own personal eternal destination? Let us choose wisely.

Lay not up for yourselves treasures upon earth ... but ... in heaven.
Matthew 6:19 and 20

Overcoming Goliath

Many of you will know of the story of David and Goliath. David, a shepherd boy, overcame Goliath, the giant champion of the Philistines, using a sling and a number of small stones. The story is a clear example of how the seemingly impossible became possible. How an apparently insignificant lad overcame huge odds, with a help of Almighty God, thereby leading the army of the Israelites to rout their enemies, the Philistines.

This story could also be a picture of you and me, and the world we live in. We probably all consider ourselves to be insignificant in terms of the world in which we live, a world full of giants such as evil, temptation, exploitation, immorality and so on.

And so we say to ourselves, 'What can I do about it all? How can I make a real difference?' David stood up against Goliath because the honour of the Lord God Almighty was at stake. Can we not do the same thing against our Goliaths? Will we?

David triumphed because the Lord God was with him. The same Lord God is with us as we stand up against His enemies – in particular the prince of darkness who seeks to lure so many people away from righteousness, uprightness and holiness.

We can defeat all our Goliaths. As the saying goes, 'The bigger they are, the harder they fall!' The Lord God of Hosts is in all those who will defend His honour, His statutes, and His holiness. And He looks for those of us who will stand in His name against the tides of wickedness. Those whose standard of holiness is not compromised by the fallen ethics of the world, and its fallen morals and values.

It's a battle cry. Are you stirred? Will you take up the cudgel? The battle may be fierce but with God we can be certain of success. He chooses the insignificant in life to confound His enemies. Let Him choose you.

O my God, I trust in Thee: let me not be ashamed, let not mine
enemies triumph over me.
Psalm 25:2

Past Your 'Sell By' Date

M y wife has noticed that foods sold in the shops appear to have increasingly shorter shelf lives. On many instances she has bought food, thinking that it will keep OK in the fridge for several days, as had happened in the past, only to find that when she went to use the food, the 'best before' date on the packs was already past and the food therefore not at its best. Even in the major shops, the 'sell by' date on food she has purchased is either the same day or the next day, so she now has to keep an eagle eye on all the dates on the packs before getting to the check-out.

The 'best before' and 'sell by' dates are I understand a relatively new requirement – by that I mean that I don't remember them there say 10 years ago but I might be mistaken, as in common with many men, my shopping expeditions have been far fewer than the ladies make ... not a good admission to make these days! As such the phrase 'past your sell-by date' has come into common language and is often used to suggest that a person, perhaps in employment terms for example, is past their best. And if you are the one spoken of, doesn't it make you feel useless and only fit for the scrap heap?

Where the things of God are concerned, discouragement is one of the favourite weapons Satan uses to get us down and keep us down. How many times have we heard in our heart, 'Of course, you'll never be any use to God ... you've been a failure from the start ... you're no good at anything ... just look at you and your problems or your character. God will never be interested in you.'

They are all lies, used to destroy our confidence in God, whom Satan detests. It doesn't matter who we are and what we may have done, it's God in us that makes the difference.

Where God is concerned, we're never past our 'sell-by date' – we don't have one. Don't be fooled into thinking otherwise.

I can do all things through Christ which strengtheneth me.
Philippians 4:13

❧

Potholes

❧

One of my son's little friends was showing me recently a scar on one of his arms, which had resulted from an accident when he was on his bicycle. It reminded me of an accident I had as a child on my own bike when, trying to carry home two boxes of shoes tied to one side of the handlebars, the bike became impossible to balance and off I came, severely grazing an arm.

After the accident my parents told me never to carry shoes on my bike again using that method and also gave me a good bit of advice regarding potholes in the road, which were fairly numerous in our village.

They said that when riding a bicycle on roads with potholes the best way to avoid them was to fix my gaze not on the potholes themselves but on a point further away and by keeping my gaze there, I would easily be able to avoid hitting the potholes in front of me. If, instead, I was to fix my gaze on the potholes themselves, I was very likely to drive towards them and be unable to avoid them.

Well, I can say that this advice seemed to work, as I don't remember any accidents with potholes during my childhood days after that. Try it for yourselves and put it to the test.

The same advice holds good for us in our Christian walk. All of us are beset from time to time with difficulties of one sort or another, and if we sit and look at the problems they only seem to get bigger and bigger until eventually we feel we cannot bypass them and avoid their effects.

Jesus says to us that if we keep our eyes on Him and not on the difficulties we shall overcome all that comes before us. The trick is not to dwell on the problem but on Jesus. He is the Master of every situation and has power to quell the strongest waves of anguish or difficulty that may threaten to overcome us.

However difficult our way may appear, or dark the clouds that hover over us, as we look to Jesus, He makes our pathway secure.

The eternal God is thy refuge, and underneath are the
everlasting arms.
Deuteronomy 33:27

❧

Pressures
❧

I have no doubt that the pressures of modern day living and of business have greatly increased over recent years, and almost everyone I speak to on this topic agrees. 'We're being asked to do more and more, with no increase in the number of staff,' is a commonly voiced concern. 'There seems to be endless re-organisation at work and we never seem to know where we are,' is another.

I believe that links between too much pressure and stress-related illnesses are well documented, and stress in turn can lead to other difficulties at work and in the home. It is a vicious circle, which can sometimes lead to despair and breakdown.

It's therefore increasingly important that we learn how to deal with the pressures of life, and in particular to be able to find time to relax and put things into perspective. We find in the Bible that Jesus, in His earthly ministry, often took time to get away from the throng and to be alone with his Father. To speak with Him and to know His prompting and His leading. It always surprises me how many of us expect as Christians to be able to live as God would have us live, without taking time to be quiet and to be in His known presence. I fear that some of us are very good talkers but are not much good at being quiet and listening.

In my experience, undue pressure can often lead to our taking an unbalanced view of things, which, in turn, can lead to our making the wrong decisions. But how can we expect to do God's will if we don't have the time or inclination to seek Him out and receive it?

In the words of a well-known hymn, 'take time to be holy.' Holiness is not like a garment that you can put on and take off at a moment's notice. It takes discipline and energy, it takes time and devotion but how much richer you are as a result.

If you haven't applied this principle before, make it one of the guiding lights that you live by.

And a highway shall be there, and a way, and it shall be
called the way of holiness.
Isaiah 35:8

Pride

Most of us have our pride, haven't we? There are many things we think, say or do that we would not wish anyone else to know about and we would be very embarrassed if others found out about them.

So we keep them to ourselves and I dare say even get to the point where we condone them in ourselves, while being critical of others who may be thinking, saying and doing the same things.

Stupid, isn't it? It's hypocrisy at its richest. And, in any event, the truth is that all the time God knows all about every thought, word and deed concerning us because he knows us altogether.

Jesus had some very strong words for these kinds of men and women. He immediately saw through those who appeared to be upright and religious people on the outside, but inside were corrupt.

Be assured that God sees and knows every part of us. He knows so well our thoughts, words and deeds – what drives us, the appearances we put on – our pride. Yet, in spite of it all, He loves us so. It was because we and those like us are this way that He sent Jesus to redeem us at such great cost. Redemption means forgiveness, repentance and a change of heart and mind and spirit to follow Him. To follow Jesus means there's no room at all for pride in us – pride of our position, of what we are, what we may look like and so on. The bottom line is that it's an abomination to God. The good news is that we can be free of it. God will deal with all of it, if we mean business.

We need to take ourselves to task before we forget how to.

Better it is to be of an humble spirit with the lowly, than to divide the spoil with the proud.
Proverbs 16:19

❧

Procrastination

❧

P rocrastination – the art of not getting things done. Aren't we good at it? We can find a hundred and one perfectly good reasons for not getting something done, but in practice we don't really want to do it, or don't know how to get it done.

The world is full of procrastinators – we even joke about it. 'The lazier a man is, the more he is going to do tomorrow.' 'A procrastinator is one who puts off until tomorrow that which he has already put off until today.'

But procrastination is a thief. It robs us of accomplishing all the things we should, and stops us succeeding in many things. It can ruin our chances of success in almost everything we try to do.

When it comes to the things of God, you'll also find procrastination. God may be calling us to a deeper and closer walk with Himself, yet we can find a multitude of what we might call 'legitimate' reasons for not obeying, and we put off fulfilling His call. 'I'll start tomorrow, I'll feel more like it then,' or ' I have this particular hindrance, so once it's gone, I'll begin.'

And who is the loser? Not only one, but possibly many others. Not just ourself by missing out on His calling, but perhaps a multitude of others whom God would have stirred through us as a result of that closer walk with Himself. Perhaps they remain outside the Kingdom of God because of our procrastination.

We may well lament the ineffectual state of the Church today – how impotent we feel it is. And yet that might just partly be so because of our own personal ineffectiveness, as a result of our procrastination.

If you haven't already done so, resign from the procrastination party with immediate effect.

And he did evil, because he prepared not his heart to
seek the Lord.
2 Chronicles 12:14

Promises

Have you looked at a bank note recently? 'I do not seem to be able to hang on to them long enough to look at them,' I can almost hear you reply. Seriously, though, they say, 'I promise to pay the bearer on demand the sum of …'

How often we have promises given to us. Even from our children, 'I promise to be good, Dad!' although sometimes the promise seems to roll off their tongues a little too easily.

From politicians to shopkeepers, we always seem to have someone making us a promise. Our washing will be whiter, this coffee will taste more like coffee or the multitude of promises included in a party's manifesto before an election. There are promises everywhere. In the wedding vows the bride and bridegroom promise that they will love, honour and cherish each other, as long as they live. Even these promises become tarnished these days for so many.

And how let down we feel when a promise is broken, when a vow is made and not kept.

You may be surprised to learn that the Bible has more than enough promises to give one for each day of the year. What is also true is that God never breaks a promise.

There is a certainty about the Word of God. There is power there, authority too, as well as promises being kept. He promised the birth of Jesus – and He came. He promised Calvary – and it happened to set mankind free, and He has promised the return of Jesus to take His people home for them to be with Him throughout eternity.

If you don't yet know God's provisions and promises for you personally, now's the time to put that right.

Whereby are given to us exceeding great and precious promises
that by these ye might be partakers of the divine nature.
2 Peter 1:4

Qualifications

I imagine that each year in many households there are sighs of relief as school and university examinations are completed and the holidays arrive.

None of us would really expect to sit and pass examinations without having studied for them, except perhaps for a few who are the 'chancers' of this world. To obtain qualifications and to become skilled in your occupation requires work and learning which only comes by application. Very few of us will become qualified just by thinking about it, dreaming about it, or telling others about it. For when the first test of our knowledge comes along, we fail dismally.

Why then do some of us apply different principles where our Christianity is concerned? Certainly, when we come to Jesus Christ and seek and find His forgiveness, know His cleansing and feel His new life within us, something has happened. We are new creatures; old things have passed away, as the Bible puts it.

But it doesn't stop there. Jesus said: 'If any one would follow me, let him deny himself and take up his cross.' The walk with Jesus is a walk of self-denial where we put Jesus first and in front of our own pursuits, our ambitions and our goals.

Some people, on receiving Christ as their personal Saviour and Lord, believe they have 'arrived.' Now that they have found the Kingdom of God, they feel they can continue to do so as they please only with the church now being part of their weekly round.

Not so. God's saints are those who have set themselves to deepen their new-found relationship with Him, to climb the high slopes of God's dwelling places and to put Him first in every aspect of life. They enter His school of obedience, His school of discipline and of self-denial.

If we are serious about our Christian walk, there are qualifications here too to be obtained.

Study to show thyself approved unto God, a workman that needeth
not to be ashamed, rightly dividing the word of truth.
2 Timothy 2:15

❧

Realising Your Inheritance

❧

I was reminded some time ago of a story where two men owned the same piece of land, one after the other. The first of these men went bankrupt and died penniless, while the other went on to make a fortune and become exceedingly wealthy, yet both had the same opportunity.

The two very different outcomes arose because there was a lot of tin in the land. The first owner never discovered this, and so never enjoyed the fruits of it. The other discovered the facts and set about mining the land to great financial benefit and gain. The tin had been there all the time, yet the first owner, who had as good a title to it as the second one, died in poverty and distress.

It is often the same with God's people. There is a spiritual treasure there for each one of us, and each one of us has the same good title to it, but for some it remains undiscovered, never enjoyed and never put to use.

If we had been asked by our employer to invest his funds to earn a good rate of return, but told him at the end of the day that we had done nothing with it, I don't think that he would be at all pleased. And if a lawyer's letter reached us advising us that we had been left a vast fortune in somebody's will, I think there would be very few, if any, of us who would not respond immediately and spend much time deciding what to do with our new-found wealth and then put our plans into action.

Jesus has already provided each one of us with a rich inheritance. Let us have the faith to be bold as His children to claim every part of it. Our lives, and the lives of those around us, will be revolutionised if we do.

The eyes of your understanding being enlightened, that ye may know what is the hope of his calling, and what (are) the riches of the glory of his inheritance in the saints.
Ephesians 1:18

Rubbish

I never cease to be amazed about just how much rubbish we collect in our household. From the beginning of a day, until the end of it, it's as if all sorts of bits and pieces are magnetically attracted to the floor, particularly the living room and the kitchen. And, of course, with children, bits and pieces from empty crisp packets and juice cartons to apple cores and drawings of this and that appear out of nowhere.

I am thankful for the efficient services of our local refuse collectors. I shudder to think at the mountain our pile of rubbish would be over a year.

That is the rubbish that goes out each week. However, like many households we also seem to collect a fair bit of this and that over the years which, if we are honest with ourselves, we have no use for, but it sounded 'a good idea at the time.'

In looking at what we do with our lives, it seems to me we also pick up unnecessary trivia on the way. We perhaps spend hours in front of the television (where has the art of communicating with each other gone?) and generally fill our lives with activities that, at the end of the day, probably distract us from the central issues of life, however sensible or fun they seemed at the time.

I wonder when life draws to a close if we will feel that while we have done so much, we may have accomplished so little.

Let's aim to clear some of the rubbish out of our living while we have the opportunity.

I count all things but loss for the excellency of the knowledge of
Christa Jesus my Lord.
Philippians 3:8

≈

Rules For Life
≈

I was particularly saddened by two reports in the newspaper. One was of a father who had killed himself and his four young children in his fume-filled car, following a recent divorce. The other concerned the death of a teenager after taking drugs at a discotheque.

'What a waste of lives, some of whom were innocent parties,' I thought. Two occasions when, in the search for happiness and fulfilment, things had gone so terribly wrong.

It still seems that rather than obey the rules we have already been given for a fulfilled and contented life, we choose to go on inventing our own ... and then we wonder why things go wrong. Young people in particular are always on the look out for the next 'experience' and will try almost anything in their quest, even although the chances that they will come upon something that works are negligible.

As a Christian, what a responsibility we have to promote the right way, indeed the only way, to find life's fulfilment. Yet how often we only present a boring imitation of what being a Christian is. According to statistics, mainstream church attendance continues to fall ... I wonder if we are really so surprised. Thank God, there are exceptions.

Without God in your life, the odds are stacked against you. Marriages are made in heaven, not on earth. And deep joy and lasting peace are not found on the discotheque floor, or in the latest designer drug. Cleanness and purity are not found in one-night stands, but heartbreak often is.

We who are Christ's, need to stand out like beacons in the night and show the real way to life, happiness and contentment. We mustn't fail our young people, when it's so obvious they need help.

Let your light so shine before men, that they may see your good works, and glorify your Father which is in heaven.
Matthew 5:16

❦

Seeing Again

❦

O ne of our neighbours had the thrill of her sight being restored after an operation. She had suffered from cataracts and had for years been unable to see clearly, with the level of her vision steadily decreasing.

As a result of the operation, she received in a moment of time, so to speak, the ability to see clearly for the first time in years. She was so pleased to be able to point out to us all the things she has been unable to see before.

In the Bible, a number of people also received their sight. Blind Bartimaeus called out to Jesus, who stopped and asked him, 'What do you want me to do for you?' Bartimaeus replied that he wanted so see, and in a moment of time he received his sight.

Then there was the healing of the blind man at Bethsaida who, when Jesus had put spittle on his eyes and put his hands on him, was able to see again.

Hearing of our neighbour's operation reminded me that while it is wonderful indeed to have your physical sight restored, what about your spiritual sight? Do we see life's issues as clearly or have we allowed scales to begin to form and slowly dull our thinking, our values, and our response to what life is really all about?

Jesus said that unless we have a spiritual rebirth, we shall not enter the Kingdom of Heaven. It's as definite as that. He said that He is the Way, and the only way, by which we can enter. Have you recognised this truth and acted upon it, or do you remain blind to it, the gods of this world blurring its reality? Or maybe you have deliberately turned yourself away from it?

God promises to restore our 'sight' relating to His Son Jesus and His Kingdom, if we, like Bartimaeus, will simply come to Him and ask Him to do so. There's a whole new world for those of us who will take that step.

I am the way, the truth and the life: no man cometh unto the Father but by me.
John 14:6

Seeing Things Clearly

A colleague of mine was peeling and scraping carrots recently and found afterwards that his actions were producing a fine carrot mist as he worked which reached up and clung to his spectacles.

He wasn't particularly aware of it at the time but began to find his vision somewhat blurred. He used the nearest fabric to him to give them a clean, but that was his clothing and it only served to smear the lenses and make matters worse.

His task finished, he carried on with a number of other duties, and it wasn't until he sat down for a cup of tea a little later, and was able to clean his spectacles properly, that he discovered how sharp and in focus the world around him looked again. It reminded me of my own school days when once a year, having visited the opticians and come out with a pair of slightly stronger lenses in my own spectacles, I marvelled at how everything became so much sharper and clearer. Those of you with excellent eyesight can count on your blessings.

Life can so easily get out of focus too, and our vision blurred. That unexpected bill which will give us difficulties in paying it, an illness in one we love or a rift in family and other relationships can all come across our path and get things out of focus.

Jesus and His Holy Spirit are the cleaning agents. If we let them touch our lives and continue to do so when things could go wrong, we shall see clearly what is right and the way to go. Jesus delights in our coming to Him like a little child and asking for his help, and His Holy Spirit pours the oil of peace and contentment across the most troubled waters.

And unto many that were blind, he gave sight.
Luke 7:21

Silence

I love the silence. It's an odd statement perhaps, but a true one. If you have to be out at work all day in the clamour of business, with telephones ringing and bosses' demands, then you'll enjoy too the sense of relief and release when the day is done, and you can retire home to peace and quiet.

Or if you're the busy housewife, there are a hundred and one things that need doing, with never a moment to yourself. We have one of these new-fangled worktop hobs with a three-speed fan above for removing all the steam, and I know my wife and I are pleased when it can be switched off, as its noise is such an intrusion.

Then if you have children, or television, or both, then you'll really know what noise is! Both can clamour for our attention, often competing with each other, slowly wearing us down to the point when we cry out for a moment's break.

So, I love the silence. The world is not very good these days at providing peace and quiet and so silence has become somewhat a luxury. The advent of pocket transistors radios, personal stereos, mobile and car telephones and so on have worked to relieve us of these precious moments. Of course, we can choose not to have any of them, but I think you'll agree that the age we live in generally has become a noisy one.

The luxury and peace of silence. Having the chance to contemplate without intrusion. To consider future hopes, and past successes and failures. And for the Christian, time to enjoy the presence of Jesus, and listen to His voice and to His words to us. Or simply to meditate upon Him who delights to call us His own.

And we rise the stronger, refreshed by His presence, strengthened in our love for Him, in our resolve to do His bidding and to speak for Him as He instructs.

Yes, I love the silence. I'd give up time and money to have more of it ... Come aside with me and know that deep inner peace and contentment that only Jesus gives as we give ourselves to Him.

In quietness and confidence shall be your strength.
Isaiah 30:15

🐦

Sin Brings Death

🐦

Coming across some schoolchildren smoking cigarettes on their way to school, I couldn't help wondering why on earth they were already at that young age into something which we now know will probably kill them, and certainly bring them all kinds of problems in later life.

But then why do people drink far too much alcohol and land up with a separate set of nasty, sometimes lethal, health problems? And those who play around in sexual terms also potentially wreak havoc with their health.

For whatever fashionable or trendy reasons, many of us, young and older, choose to ignore the consequences of our actions.

The Bible is clear and unequivocal about these things. 'The soul that sins, it shall surely die', we read. And so it is. Sin brings havoc into our lives in so many ways, and yet we choose to ignore the warning signs. Sin should carry a health warning. But there is one. Our consciences. They do tell us when we're about to do wrong, they nudge us to do the right thing. They trouble us when we have done the wrong thing and need to put matters right.

We reap the consequences of our actions. And that is also true for those of us who seek only to do good, who seek the blessing of God on what they do, and who follow the Lord Jesus, wheresoever He takes them. Into these lives comes a different set of consequences, which include a deep settled peace, an abundant joy and everlasting life with Christ Himself. That's what God wants for all of us.

Repent ye therefore and be converted, that your sins may be
blotted out.
Acts 3:19

Small But Effective

Knowing my interest in office gadgets, one of my children showed me a new pocket stapler he had bought from the stationers. It was so small it looked like a large bug, but he had tested it out and told me it worked very well.

Small but effective. Each of us is one inhabitant among over 5,500,000,000 individuals who populate the globe, never mind the countless varieties of animals, fish, birds and plants that live alongside us. When you see it in these terms, the world is a miraculous place, with a limitless Creator.

It's also a miracle that in all of this creation, God has such a personal care and interest in us as individuals. He knows us altogether, and wants to be involved in every detail of our lives.

We might feel that as one tiny speck of humanity, how can we ever do anything of real importance for good, for humanity, or for God? I thought about the words that described the stapler... small but effective. And about how effective we can be for God. Perhaps more importantly, how effective God wants us to be for Him. I had the privilege of knowing one lady who lived locally, a small and apparently insignificant lady, but a hugely effective servant of God in her community and beyond. The call of God was on her life and she followed that call to the letter. And many, many individuals have reaped the benefit of her ministry in their own lives, I amongst them.

Small and effective. To keep ourselves out of the picture in order that God can work out His miracles through us. It's a huge call, and such an important one.

Don't ever think that your life is unimportant ... either to God or to His creation. Put yourself in His hands and you will discover just how important you are to Him, and through Him to others.

The effectual fervent prayer of a righteous man availeth much.
James 5:16

Suddenly Clear

I have been a contact lens wearer for a long number of years and have been fortunate in finding them both easy and helpful to wear. I am not the world's best cleaner of lenses and really should do better, particularly in view of the potential health risks to my eyes of the lenses not being kept scrupulously clean. Mind you, if you're as short-sighted as I am, there is not a little humour in trying to keep your lenses clean, as taking them out means you've great difficulty in seeing the lenses at all, never mind cleaning them!

However, what a difference cleaning them thoroughly can make. Suddenly, everything is so much clearer again, and can be seen as it is, not as you see it in distorted fashion through your lenses in their unclean state.

I find that many of us go through life puzzling over this problem or that one, wondering why things happen, or are allowed to happen, and never feeling satisfied with the conclusions we reach. Many Christians too often seem not to be sure what their calling in God is and what the future holds for them. These questions seem to tantalise with certainty never apparently attainable.

That is, until God speaks to us. His Holy Spirit applies the eye-salve of the Master's Voice and the authority of His word to us. And it all becomes suddenly clear and definite, and we are left in no doubt.

God speaks to us today, just as He spoke to Moses, Elijah and to so many others. The Bible is full of His word and His promises to us. Promises for our good, promises that are for eternity, and promises that He will not break. So if you're one of those who are still unclear as to His purposes for you personally, go searching, and listen for the Voice that makes everything so clear.

My sheep hear my voice, and I know them, and they follow me.
John 10:27

Taking The Plunge

&

Most of us can remember occasions when we were faced with a particular event and, after remaining rather hesitant for a while, we finally 'took the plunge' to find that our doubts were unnecessary and fears groundless. In fact we wish we had launched into the matter earlier.

Perhaps for some of us, marriage might be an example of what I mean. I know many people who had last minute jitters about the impending ceremony and commitment but took the plunge and never looked back.

It might have been a new job involving added responsibility, or a move to another part of the country or abroad. Or the purchase of a new house or car or a change of school for the children. You will be able to find other examples relating to your own life.

I can remember, as a small boy, standing at the edge of what seemed as very large swimming pool, being rather shy of approaching the question of learning how to swim. But after having careful instruction and literally taking the plunge, it all changed and I learned to enjoy swimming very much.

Do we approach the Christian life in much the same way? We may realise that a commitment to Jesus Christ will mean putting the control of our lives into the hands of another, resulting in a different way of life with different values and different priorities. Perhaps we stand on the outside, as it were, looking in, a little hesitant and wondering what is involved.

Then God speaks to us and we come to Him. And all our fears and wonderings disappear, replaced with the deep settled peace of God's Holy Spirit in our lives. Our relationship begins to deepen with Jesus and we realise that we can, with confidence, entrust him with every detail of our lives.

Maybe you've 'taken the plunge' and found this Jesus. Or perhaps you are still on the edge, outside the knowledge of His love and care for you individually. Let me encourage you to take the next step and invite Him into your life. You will not be disappointed.

Commit thy way unto the Lord, trust also in him, and he shall
bring it to pass.
Psalm 37:5

❧

The Garden Tomb

❧

As part of a trip to Israel, I had the opportunity of visiting the Garden Tomb in Jerusalem, which some evidence suggests could be the burial place of Jesus.

Jerusalem is a bustling noisy city, comprising both Arabs and Jews, and a very large number of tourists who visit this part of the Holy Land. For these reasons, and to avoid large numbers of tourist groups, we visited the Garden Tomb early in the morning, at about 8 o'clock. On our arrival we were immediately struck with the quietness and serenity of the garden, which includes the Tomb, and from which the suggested place of Jesus' crucifixion can be seen.

It was like being in an oasis in a desert place and we were able to drink in the peace and quietness as we looked and remembered the life, death and resurrection of Jesus. We sat for sometime, reliving all that had happened nearly 2000 years ago, and let His peace come upon us and refresh us.

I'm sure it's true that most of us today have to live our lives in the midst of noise and activity and we can be pulled this way and that way with so many things clamouring for our attention. But I wonder, just as we discovered that overwhelming sense of peace at the Garden Tomb, whether we realise that we can have such peace in our hearts as part of our daily lives.

This peace also comes from Jesus. From accepting Him as Saviour and Lord of our life, and receiving His forgiveness for our wrongdoing. His peace in our hearts enables us to live our lives as He directs, whatever our circumstances might be.

Do we know this peace? Or are we tossed about from day to day with no firm foundations, anxious over many things, perhaps scarred by the effects of hurts we have received at the hand of others?

Come and find His peace-peace 'that passes all our understanding' as the Bible describes it. Peace to be calm in the midst of storm, and quiet where there is a tumult around you.

You will never be the same again.

And the peace of God, which passeth all understanding, shall keep your hearts and minds through Christ Jesus.
Philippians 4:7

❦

The Goldfish Bowl

❦

I have bumped into goldfish on a few occasions - not literally of course. Usually in a home where two goldfish were swimming about in a traditional goldfish bowl.

Whether they were contented or not, I do not know. They didn't tell me. I don't know anything at all about the size of goldfish brains, or whether they actually are aware of their surroundings, or the fact that they are swimming about in endless circles not really getting anywhere.

I also don't imagine they are aware of the possibilities of swimming free in a river stream in rich and varied countryside with all the changing temperatures and weather conditions our country offers, and the sense of real freedom that might bring to them. Swimming alongside all kinds of greenery, reeds and bushes, meeting many other fishes and river creatures along the way. No doubt it's safer in their little bowl.

Swimming around in circles and getting nowhere. Might that sum up our existence too? Caught up in the humdrum of life and not knowing anything different. Never knowing that there is much more to life than that.

We can break free. We are created in the image of God, we read in the Bible. Created to live a miraculous life, full of power, of joy and of freedom from all fears imaginable.

It's time to see beyond our goldfish bowl … to reach out for all that God has for us, and to find all that is in Him.

If the Son therefore shall make you free, ye shall be free indeed.
John 8:36

The Hearing Ear

Most of us are blessed with good hearing. As in many other things, children and young people seem to have particularly sharp hearing, if my own children are anything to go by. They can hear the sweetie jar being opened from two rooms away, and are by my side before the lid is replaced!

There again, sometimes we only listen to what we really want to hear. There are many apparently 'deaf' people when it comes to being asked to go an errand or do something they have been asked to do on a number of previous occasions.

All of us too have what I might call 'an inner ear.' I'm sure you know what I mean. With our 'inner ear' we may listen to all the voices around us, this advice or that advice, and then decide what to do. Perhaps we ignore proper advice and go our own way regardless.

For the Christian too, all sorts of voices clamour for our attention, perhaps particularly one that would entice us from our walk with God. But those who have found Jesus and know the sound of His voice have learned to tune our inner ear, or spirit, to God's Spirit to hear what He is saying to us, not being prepared to trust our own judgement. And God does speak very clearly and very specifically to us in this way.

With all other voices shut out, we can have real communion with the Lord we love, knowing the sweetness of His voice, as he tells us of things concerning Himself and His Kingdom, and concerning ourselves.

Have you heard the Voice of God speaking to you personally? Perhaps you have shrugged it off and not responded. Perhaps you were not sure whom it was speaking to you. Perhaps you put it down to your own imagination.

God wants to claim our attention. He wants to speak to us about eternal issues, about heaven and hell, about his Son Jesus, about His love for us. Let us tune our spiritual 'inner ear' to Him and hear what He has to say to us. It will only be for our good.

Give ye ear, and hear my voice: hearken and hear my speech.
Isaiah 28:23

The Impact Of Christ

I was speaking with a friend who was describing to me the attitude of his employers to the voluntary activities he was keen to do more of. Their reaction was one of praise for his initiative and drive, and encouragement to go on with it, but on the basis that it didn't impact on them and his work for them.

That's just how some of us deal with the claims of Jesus. Our response to His invitation to follow Him could be one of 'OK, but only on the basis that it doesn't impact on what I want to do or to be!' 'Well, I'm prepared to go to church, and try to be nice to others and live a reasonable life, but don't ask me to be more radical than that.'

When Jesus does come into your life, it is radical … it's life changing. We are converted and the meaning of converted is to be turned around. All of life changes. The power and the life of God come into us and life takes on a completely new meaning with old aims and ambitions dying away as Christ comes. Life becomes so new and so exciting. The power of the gospel is ours. The inheritance God has for us personally can be realised. All His treasures have our name on them. How can you stand still when the God of all the universe is within you?

Let the Spirit of God into your life and then try and go about your ordinary business without being radically changed. You won't make it. Every blade of grass seems to sparkle when seen through His eyes … His freshness is everywhere.

Don't put any 'pre-conditions' in the way.

Be strong in the Lord, and in the power of his might.
Ephesians 6:10

The Inner Man

In our department stores there are such a variety of clothes on display – every shape and size catered for in every colour, it seems, with plenty to tempt the money from our pockets. These stores are very busy places with people looking at the latest fashions, trying on the various designs and checking out the newest brand names.

It doesn't need much imagination to see how fashion-conscious people are and how important being in the style of the moment is to so many, with a lot of money involved in this pursuit.

How differently Jesus views these things. He isn't so interested in the outward things, the trappings we might call them, but in the inner parts of a person.

It doesn't matter who we are, what we look like, how much money we have (or how little), who our parents are and so on – Jesus is interested in the inner person. He didn't die on Calvary to make us rich, or to provide material things – He died to make a way whereby we might know God and be reconciled to Him. And to fill us with His life, His peace and His joy – worth much, much more than anything money can buy.

If you feel God knocking on the door of your heart and seeking to be involved in your life, your hopes and your doubts, open the door to him and invite Him in. He is always ready for that invitation.

And rend your heart, and not your garments, and turn unto the
Lord your God: for he is gracious and merciful, slow to
anger, and of great kindness.
Joel 2:13

The Missing Day

🐾

Some time ago, space scientists in America were trying to determine the position of the sun, moon and stars 100 years and 1,000 years from now. In order to do this they had to plot the orbits through past centuries.

They ran a computer measurement back and forth over the centuries and suddenly it came to a halt, as the computer signalled that something was wrong with the measurement. Nothing was technically wrong, but the computer indicated that a day was missing in elapsed time. The scientists were dumbfounded. There appeared no answer.

After some time, one of the scientists remembered a reference in the Bible to the sun standing still. On checking, they found in the book of Joshua a pretty ridiculous statement for anybody with 'common sense', or so they thought. Joshua was concerned because he was surrounded by the enemy and if darkness fell, they would overpower him. So Joshua asked the Lord to make the sun stand still. And it did, and didn't go down for nearly 24 hours.

The scientists checked their computers and found that this was the answer, and yet not quite. The time that was missing in Joshua's day was 23 hours and 20 minutes ... not a whole day. And 40 minutes had to be found because in projecting space orbits, it would be multiplied many times over.

Again, one of the scientists remembered that somewhere in the Bible the sun went backwards (in the second chapter of 2nd Kings, in the Old Testament). Hezekiah, on his deathbed, was visited by the prophet Isaiah, who told him he was not going to die. Hezekiah did not believe him and looked for proof by asking that, as a sign, the sun would go backwards 10 degrees, which it did. 10 degrees is 40 minutes and so the scientists were able to enter these times and chart the orbits successfully.

This isn't fantasy – it's literally true. And the God who worked wonders in the days of Joshua and Isaiah still works wonders today

... for you and for me.
Thou art the God that doest wonders: thou hast declared thy
strength among the people.
Psalm 77:14

The New Birth

I remember well the day my wife and I, together with our young children, were visiting some close friends, and had the delight of seeing for the first time their new baby daughter.

We had a great time with them seeing photographs of the baby taken when only a few weeks old. Our children also had fun talking and playing with the baby, giving her the odd prod or two.

The birth of a baby really is such a miracle with each feature perfectly formed so that the baby can grow into a healthy child and adult. And, of course, there is the joy of holding your child, and nurturing it throughout the days and years ahead. A new birth can also be a stirring occasion, this springing forth of a new life into the family. And it so clearly depicts another 'new life', which is ours when we come to Jesus and claim Him as our Lord.

Jesus said, 'Except a man be born again, he shall not see the Kingdom of Heaven.' Now Jesus didn't mean being physically born again, but the coming of His new life within us. A life of power, of love, of peace and of security, as we are born into the family of God.

Does it sound strange, or just wishful thinking? Well, there are countless millions who can say with certainty that they have experienced this new life from Jesus. It brings a cleansing of all that is wrong in our lives, a dying away of old habits, an infilling of

God's Spirit within us, with new thoughts, new desires and a new priority for all of our living. For without Jesus Christ in our lives, they are empty, 'dead in trespass and sin' as the Bible puts it. And that deadness leads to everlasting separation from Him. So if you are still to do so, discover this new birth for yourself. You'll be markedly different when you do.

I tell you the truth; no one can see the kingdom of God
unless he is born again.
John 3:3

❧

The 'Too Difficult' Drawer
❧

I wonder how often many of us have invented what I might call a 'too difficult' drawer as part of our living. As a particular example, I well remember in one of the offices where I worked, a fair number of letters, other correspondence, and requests for attention relating to thorny problems coming before us, and the more difficult of these seemed to lie for a long time before being dealt with. And when they rose to the top of the pile they were relegated back to the bottom, or temporarily filed in the 'too difficult' or 'not for today' or the 'needs detailed examination' file in the desk drawer.

The same principle can also apply in other areas of life. We know we need to deal with particular issues, often relating to other people and our relationships with them, but they look too difficult to face, and so we relegate them to the back of our minds and say to ourselves, 'I'll deal with them later,' but later never comes around.

The well known saying 'Never put off to tomorrow what you can do today' well applies.

And when it comes to God and His relationship with us, or perhaps the lack of it, many of us start to stall. While knowing that we should consider these issues, we put them off for a 'more appropriate time', we tell ourselves, hoping the feeling we have that we should do something will pass away.

What we don't realise is that God wants to deal with these issues of life to sort them, to put the bad parts away for ever and to enable us to find our lives in Him, and know His goodness, kindness, love and mercy filling us over and over again.

If you're feeling a bit uncomfortable where the things of God are concerned, and feeling that you really should get to know Him better than you do, now's the time to take action. God will meet you fully every step you take towards Him.

Is anything too hard for the Lord?
Genesis 18:14

The Vital Ingredient

There is nothing more galling than running out of petrol. Fortunately, it has only happened to me once, but it was very frustrating when I realised that I would not make my destination on time and I needed to sit and wait for one of the motorway rescue services to come to my aid. What made matters worse was that I had run out of petrol only a mile from a service station, having already travelled some 250 miles that day.

There is something rather futile about sitting in a vehicle, perhaps a very expensive one, full of components and gadgets, knowing that it is missing the one vital ingredient that it needs to be able to fulfil its purpose. And no other ingredient would have helped. Petrol, and only petrol, was what was required.

There are many other examples in life where one missing vital ingredient can result in futility. For example, a football match with 22 players, a referee, his assistants and other officials would be of no use if there were no ball. No matter how many other ingredients you have, a cake needs an oven in which to bake it. A bicycle is pretty useless without its chain. A loveless marriage does no one any favours. The list goes on and on ...

The same truth also applies to us as individuals. We are more than flesh and bones – we are spiritual beings with a soul and spirit. And just as my car needed the vital ingredient of petrol, our lives are bankrupt without God in them. He, and only He is the vital ingredient that changes us from a fallen, sin-wrecked people into those who know His Presence and His Holy Spirit within us where the ordinary becomes the miraculous and where our quality of life in Him soars far, far above what it is without Him.

Essentially, we cannot fulfil our personal destinies on our own. God is the vital ingredient from which purpose of life flows, where purity and love have their beginnings and endings, and with whom our lives can know peace as a deep, settled pool within us.

If this vital ingredient is missing in your life, now's the time for change.

I am the bread of life: he that cometh to me shall never hunger,
and he that believeth in me shall never thirst.
John 6:35

The Wrong Way

I firmly believe that there can be no-one as obstinate as the male driver taking his passengers out in the car, aiming for a particular destination.

A friend was telling me of an occasion where the husband was driving his wife and friends to a town some distance away. The driver missed a turning, to the increasing disquiet of his passengers.

'Are you sure this is the right road? enquired his wife, a little nervously. 'Of course it is,' her husband replied confidently, and so they sped on. However, the questions continued, somewhat to his irritation, while he (privately) gazed hopefully for known landmarks on the journey.

On they went as he muttered to himself, 'I'm sure this is the way' when he was in fact not sure at all. And eventually he stopped the car at the side of the road and having to swallow his pride he admitted sheepishly, 'I'm afraid we're lost.' So they retraced their route until they discovered where they had gone wrong, and finally reached their destination.

This story made me smile, but it also provides a very true illustration of our lives and of our need of Jesus.

Many people set out in life confidently, saying, 'I have no need of Jesus in my life; I'll make out all right.' But as life's journey begins to unravel, mistakes are made, wrong decisions are taken, and we begin to lose our way.

Perhaps, at first, we refuse to admit it to ourselves - indeed I imagine many people have gone to the grave without acknowledging their need of Jesus, but for some of us, the realisation comes upon us that our lives are not right and that we have lost our way. The Bible says we are indeed lost, but that Jesus provides the way, and the only way, to life as it is supposed to be.

'I am the way, the truth and the life,' Jesus says, and those who put their trust in Him find that to be entirely true.

There is a way which seemeth right unto a man, but the end
thereof are the ways of death.
Proverbs 14:12

Time

I'm sure that most of us feel that so often the one thing we lack is time. Whatever our own personal situation, life is lived at such a hectic pace these days, with so much demanding our attention, that we never seem to have enough time for all that is required of us.

It's perhaps ironic that with so many labour-saving devices in our homes and at our work, we still have so little time to spare. But then, perhaps it is because we have filled our lives with so much, that we have so little time to accomplish it all.

Perhaps our desire for material wealth, a new home or a better job, is taking up too much of our thoughts and time. Perhaps it is our desire for sport or fun that takes us out and about with hardly any time to stop and think. It may even be that we would not know what to do with ourselves if we actually did have time on our hands.

Are our hearts so taken up with the things of this world that we have no time for the things of God? Have we become slaves to our jobs, or to the upkeep of our homes, our gardens, of our cars, even our bodies?

These are hard words. But Jesus also said that we cannot serve two masters – we can love only one to the detriment of the other.

We need to take time to be holy. Time to know Jesus, to be in His presence, and to hear His voice speaking to us individually.

My presence shall go with thee, and I will give thee rest.
Exodus 33:14

Tinkering With The Peripheries

I don't know much about car engines, or any other kind of engine for that matter, but I do know that for an engine to run well, all the parts must be operating smoothly and in harness with each other. If not, as I know to my cost, you get a coughing, spluttering car, which refuses to go even the shortest distance without major difficulty.

If the engine is not in tune and running smoothly, then no amount of tinkering elsewhere on the car will help. Polishing the chrome or the windscreen is absurd. Tightening the wheel nuts or filling up the windscreen washer will not do much either! You need to get down to the problem itself and sort what is wrong, before there will be an improvement.

The truth of this is clear to see when it comes to car engines, but, alas, not so clear when it comes to us. The Bible tell us clearly that we are all sinners, and in need of the touch and forgiveness of Jesus in our lives. That's the major fault, and no amount of tinkering about on the peripheries of life will help or change it. Changing the clothes we wear does not change the person inside. Polishing our image doesn't change matters either. We need to get down to the real problem.

And, just like me when it comes to cars, we cannot sort the problem ourselves. We need a friend who can, and in this case there is only one such Friend. But not only can Jesus help, He wants to, and is ready to. We need to call Him. We need to ask Him to come over. We need to let Him get at the problem and take the necessary action to sort it.

Don't deal at the peripheries. Go to the heart of the matter and get help that is effective.

Draw nigh unto God and he will draw nigh unto you.
James 4:8

Toothache

Ilone of us likes toothache. Those amongst you who suffer most from this affliction will readily agree. Toothache almost always starts up at the most unsuitable time – when we're away from home, or at the weekend when the dentists are closed or just when we're going to bed and looking forward to a good night's sleep.

Yet many of us, when it comes to facing the dentist's chair, find all kinds of excuses why our toothache's (suddenly!) not that bad, and why there is no real need to go to the dentist right away. After all, he's probably too busy anyway! The word dentist can produce an unnatural fear amongst many of us who would rather suffer for days than face a visit which, for all that, is likely to solve the problem quickly and effectively. So we put up with our toothache despite the pain.

For the Christian, too, when it comes to being free from sin and its effects, I fear that many of us adopt the same stance. Instead of coming to Jesus and letting Him deal with all that is wrong, we only see it from our point of view, and prefer to suffer without a remedy. Sin is rather like toothache – it nags away at you, spoiling the quality of life you could have, without offering anything in return.

So why do we allow ourselves to live an impoverished Christian life? Perhaps only because we are scared of the cost. We look at things one-sidedly, fearful of what to expect. It does not have to be that way; the Holy Spirit will give us the will to change, if we want to.

Or will we stay with our toothache forever?

It is the Lord. Let him do what seemeth him good.
1 Samuel 3:18

Turned Aside

Now if you are a parent with children at home, or have been one, I expect that you will sympathise with me when I mention the difficulties sometimes in asking children to do something and the problems they seem to have in carrying out our requests.

'Yes, Mum. OK. I'll do it in just a minute.' And minutes have an enormous elasticity – some last for at least half an hour and others go into never-never time!

Or, when the children appear, without having done what was requested, it's because … 'Oh, sorry … I was going to do it, but got caught up in reading this book.' Or … 'Ooops … I meant to do it, but forgot all about it when my pal appeared.'

Don't they get all too easily sidetracked and forget the task in hand! Some of us as parents are not perfect either. How easily we can forget some of the promises we make.

We can also let it happen all too easily with God, I fear. We mean to carry out His instructions, but something always seems to get in the way, deliberately on our part or otherwise. And the high and holy calling that God has for us, and the practical outworking of His purposes for us, don't take place … and then we wonder why God doesn't seem to be interested in us or doesn't appear to answer our prayers.

Obedience, especially to God, is vital if we are to accomplish all that is there for us. It's a difficult word these days, not liked by many and practised by relatively few. Don't allow yourself to get sidetracked by anything that could get in the way of God's highest for you. If you and they only knew it, other lives are depending upon you not to falter.

He that abideth in me, and I in him, the same bringeth forth much
fruit: for without me ye can do nothing.
John 15:5

Unchangeable

My young son was very upset to learn that, because of the way leap years arrive, his birthday would not be on a Saturday. He was most put out and demanded that his Dad do something about it!

While in his son's eyes Dad could fix most things, this was one he couldn't, and so Dad had to explain that he was unable to change the leap year difficulty and that there were some things in life which just couldn't be altered. Nevertheless, because his birthday fell on a Sunday that year, they could celebrate it on the Saturday anyway.

The principle is true. There are some things in life that, no matter how we may want to, and no matter how hard we try, we cannot change. Spiritual principles are the same. Sin is sin. Wrongdoing is wrongdoing. And God hates sin.

We may try and convince Him that what we are doing is not all that bad, and certainly not as bad as our neighbour is doing, but the fact remains that if it's wrong, its wrong, and deep down we will know it. We may try and get Him to change His mind, or see our point of view – but it will be to no avail. God knows sin and how it destroys us – His hatred of it is immovable. His love for us is also immovable. He loves us so much that it cost Him His Son Jesus who, by His death, paid the price once and for all for all our iniquity, so we can walk away from its penalty.

It's the greatest love story known to man. And we, individually, can all participate in it by knowing Jesus personally. It's us He wants to know. Not our neighbour, our friends, our colleagues at work. No – it's us. So reach out and touch Him. You'll never be the same again and your life will change – that's another principle that's unshakeable and proved by millions.

Come now, and let us reason together, saith the Lord: though your sins be as scarlet, they shall be as white as snow; though they be red like crimson, they shall be as wool.
Isaiah 1:18

Unwanted Baggage

I happened to be away for a few days at a conference, which meant packing two small cases and some suits to take with me in the car. I arrived at the conference hotel some hours later and was not able to park at or near the front door of the hotel, having to park some distance away at the rear of the building.

This meant me lugging both cases and my suits from the car round the hotel foyer, which I accomplished with some effort, with their shape, weight and size leaving me feeling a little sore. I duly got up to my hotel room and with quite a sense of relief was very pleased to be able to put all the items down and know that I would not require to lift them all again until the end of my stay. I thought of how awkward it would be if I had to carry all these items around with me during my stay at the hotel and throughout the conference.

In another sense I know that any of us do carry a lot of 'baggage' around with us, perchance over many, many years. Baggage like little or major hurts we have picked up at the hands of others, or guilt, fears and frustrations which cling to us, or jealousies and anger which boil up inside us from time to time. All this baggage weighs us down, making us feel 'down' and tired, and thinking that life will never be any different in the future.

Is that you? Are you carrying a load which weighs you down, with apparently no likelihood of relief and release?

One of the main reasons Jesus came was to set us free from all these burdens and cares. It's a wonderful feeling knowing you're free. Knowing that He has taken the power of them from you. And in their place filled you with His own peace and security.

He will release us from them if we ask Him to.

Come unto me, all ye that labour and are heavy laden,
and I will give you rest.
Matthew 11:28

What Have You Done With Your Life?

O n occasions I have taken to reading the major obituaries which fill up a page each day in one of our national newspapers. Not because I have a morbid interest in death, but rather that because of my own advancing years, I find I know an increasing number of those whose obituaries appear.

Many whose details appear in the page have filled their lives with a great deal, and have done much for their country and their fellows in terms of job achievement, military service and social improvements. But, for all that, one inescapable fact constantly strikes me. While many, if not all of them, may have achieved much, if they have never met and acknowledged and followed the Lord Jesus Christ, their lives will have missed so much and will have been empty by comparison.

I well remember a senior colleague of mine who, approaching retirement, said to me: 'I've got the nice house, the executive car, the yacht, a lovely family, luxury holidays and so on, but you know, deep down inside, I'm empty.'

It's true – you can gain the whole world, as the Bible put it, but lose your soul, the most vital part of you. We can never be complete outside of a relationship with Jesus; never know that real sense of peace and security and of lasting happiness that comes from knowing Him.

Even if we've accomplished what appears to be very little in the world's eyes, the truth remains that we can be complete in Jesus – we have no need for anything else. Let's not get to the end of *our* road without discovering Jesus and all He has for us.

And ye are complete in him.
Colossians 2:10

What Will You Do With Your Life?

I was travelling in the car, coming home from dropping off a friend and thinking about a number of issues of the day, when I passed alongside a large cemetery and saw a mass of graves and headstones in front of me.

The thought flashed into my mind 'Well, if I was there, I wouldn't be able to do anything about anything', for my life would be gone with no further time to change anything, be it past, present or future.

The old saying, 'You've only got one life to live,' is true. You don't have a second chance to live the past over again. And perhaps many of us wish we could, for we wouldn't do a second time what we have done, and we would do a lot that we haven't done.

The truth is that while there's life in us, we can start afresh. God calls out to each one of us to follow Him. It's a call to action. To make our lives count for Him. To wield His sword and cut through all that is false in life, all that deludes and deceives by promising so much and delivering so little.

However, if our lives are dead to His call, 'dead in trespass and sin' as the Bible puts it, we are, like those in the cemetery, of no value to His cause. There is something rather sad looking at a life which could have done so much, yet through its own folly or waywardness has achieved so little. Let's make sure our life is not like that. God's call to you and me is always strong and clear. The opportunity is there. We miss it at our peril.

I am come that they might have life, and that they might
have it more abundantly.
John 10:10

Words

I've been listening to a lot of words these days. I seem to have been inundated by telephone calls from companies offering cheaper gas or electricity; I've also been to a few places where there has been non stop chatting, and to some presentations where one presenter after another offered words of information, explanation and encouragement.

Mind you, those who know me well will tell you that I am not above being able to offer words myself, and not a few of them, when the occasion warrants it or even when it doesn't.

I would be interested to know how many words on average we listen to over a lifetime, and how many we speak ourselves. Some of us may have spoken a lot more then we have listened to!

The English language has many lovely words, others most expressive, and some all too regularly used which would be better left unspoken. Words spoken can be as damaging as the sharpest rapier, wounding for a lifetime. Others can be soothing to a troubled heart.

But the most electric of words are the words which bring us life. Jesus spoke these kinds of words. His words literally brought the dead back to life, they healed people of all kinds of dreadful diseases; they had the authority to remove the guilt and stain of sinfulness and the power to comfort those who mourned.

How many words of power and authority will you hear over the next week or two? Will the words of Jesus come into your heart and bring forth new life in you? And through how many of us who are God's children will come His words of life to others? These are the words that matter. They bring life, hope, happiness and health.

If ye abide in me, and my words abide in you, ye shall ask what ye will, and it shall be done unto you.
John 15:7

Worry

Worrying is an awful business. It so easily upsets your equilibrium, it can drive you to distraction, it can even break up families. And yet so many of us just can't stop worrying.

Worry can be a killer too. I have read that over half of 45-year-old Americans in business have to undergo treatment for the effects of stress and worry. And many people are cut off in the prime of their lives as a result of heart attacks or other illnesses related to worry and stress.

Yet almost all the things we worry about never actually come to pass. Some of us even worry about having nothing to worry about. It's a desperate business.

We worry about how we look. We worry about our jobs. We worry about losing our jobs. We worry whether we are any good at our jobs. We worry about what people think about us. We worry about the safety of our children. We worry about our health, or lack of it. We worry about the yesterdays and tomorrows of our lives.

The list seems almost endless.

Is this the way it's meant to be? Is an integral part of life worrying? I don't believe it should be or needs to be that way.

I suggest to you that a lot of our worrying is as a result of insecurity. The human race needs to feel loved. We need to feel safe and, you know, once the love of God enters into a person's life, it takes the place of all the worries. Jesus calms our troubles and quells our fears. He replaces them with His own love and peace. Peace that is beyond our wildest dreams. It is deeper than anything we can imagine. Perfect peace, as the Bible puts it.

Whatever your circumstances, He will bring calm where there is storm, He will bring peace where there is turbulence and He will destroy any hold that worrying has over you.

Peace I leave with you, my peace I give unto you: not as the world giveth, give I unto you. Let not your heart be troubled, neither let it be afraid.
John 14:27